Gunild Keetman

ELEMENTARIA

First acquaintance with Orff-Schulwerk

Edition 11152

Drawings: Ottmar Frick, Reutlingen

Photographs: Peter Keetman

Carl Orff

In remembrance of over four decades of collaboration

Contents

Part One: Rhythmic-Melodic Exercises

Part Two: Elementary Movement Training

Appendix

Abbreviations used in the text:

acc.	accompaniment
AG.	alto glockenspiel
AM.	alto metallophone
AX.	alto xylophone
BD.	bass drum
BX.	bass xylophone
C.	child
Chn.	children
Cl.	clapping
Clav.	claves
Cym.	cymbal(s)
F.	fingers
Glk.	glockenspiel
Gr.	group
Ind.	Indian bells (finger cymbals)
Mar.	maracas (or other soft rattle or shaker)
Pa.	patschen
Rec.	Recorder (usually descant)
SB.	sleigh bells
SD.	side drum
SG.	soprano glockenspiel
SM.	soprano metallophone
Sn.	finger-snapping
St.	stamping
SX.	soprano xylophone
T.	teacher
Tam.	tambourine
Th.	base of thumb
Timp.	timpani
Tr.	tambour
Tri.	triangle
Wb.	woodblock
Xyl.	xylophone

Abbreviations used in the movement section:

b.	backwards
bef.	(before) a cross-over step—foot concerned moves across in front of the other
beh.	cross-over step—foot concerned moves across behind the other
f.	forwards
jp.	jump
l.	left
out	r. or l. foot steps out sideways
r.	right
tog.	r. or l. foot closes in to the other
tog. tog.	r. or l. foot closes in to the other without a transfer of weight

Preface

This book sets out to lay the foundations for practical work with Orff-Schulwerk, particularly in its earliest stages, and to help the teacher to develop his own imagination. He should thereby discover the educational value of Orff-Schulwerk for himself. This will help him not to fall into a routine, but rather to transmit the basic material in his own way.

The different areas of work are here separated and placed consecutively, but in the classroom these should be combined with one another in a meaningful way. This applies not only to the two parts of the book but also to the various sub-divisions, each one of which starts with the most simple material. It should also be taken into consideration that material, handled in this book in a few, short extracts, should in practice extend over a longer period of time.

Before he starts to teach, the teacher should have gained an overall picture of the whole range of activity. It is also particularly important that he should proceed slowly and that he should be continually presenting the fundamental matter in new and varied forms.

For advice and inspiration during the preparation of this book I should like particularly to thank Suse Böhm and Werner Thomas.

Diessen/Ammersee, July 1969

G. K.

Introduction

This book is a fundamental, practical handbook for Orff-Schulwerk. It answers the questions that teachers ask themselves when they first become acquainted with the material, its selection, organisation, didactic preparation and methodical presentation.

When 'Music for Children' was first formulated about twenty years ago the work started with children of about seven years old. Now, in line with the most recent knowledge about early education, it often begins in nursery or infant school. It was therefore necessary to build an 'underneath extension' or rather a 'substructure'. A fundamental initiation is of course essential when beginning to work with *every* age group, for the suitability of the practical foundations for music making is far from dependent upon age. With older children only the choice of text will change and the possibility of a quicker rate of progress exist. The tempo and intensity at which one works will be determined by many factors: the difference in reaction between town and country children; the size of a class or group; the possibility of daily or only weekly music making; the attitude of the teacher to the question: Is Orff-Schulwerk 'fundamental' or 'supplementary' to my teaching?; the available amount of space for movement teaching; the instrumental equipment; the present state of motivation—whether a group will be more captivated and encouraged through singing, speech work or movement, and many other reasons will bring about a continually varied choice of material and style of teaching.

A classification of material according to age or grade, subject matter and curricula, as is so frequently attempted, is therefore as impossible as it is absurd. A saying, a riddle, a piece of weather lore is as impossible to pin down to a particular age group as is a short poem by Bert Brecht* ('Der Rauch' (The smoke) perhaps). The choice and appropriate use of even the simplest material is left to the educational instinct and intellectual range of the person teaching. Therefore, for example, when first embarking on Schulwerk with adolescents, preference will be given to speech work with suitable texts and to work with instruments of the wind and drum families (trumpet, timpani and other drums).

The poetic quality of the texts, however, is decisive at all age levels if they are to be educationally productive. Infantile baby-talk, bad verses and inferior pieces that are slovenly and devoid of every poetic intention; these abound in 'artistic' education as can be learnt from a fleeting glance at the

*An equivalent in the English language would be 'The fog' by Carl Sandburg. (M. M.)

supermarket offering music for young players and amateur plays. F. M. Böhme's warning in 1876 against 'Schulversuchen für die Kleinen' (school experiments for the little ones) and 'schreckbaren Kindergärtner-Unpoesie' (frightful kindergarten unpoetry) is still valid.

In the realm of German traditional children's songs his collection *Deutsches Kinderlied und Kinderspiel* is the inexhaustible standard work from which most of the texts for the early stages of Orff-Schulwerk are taken.* It shows the riches of many regions in its various dialects. 'Dialect in children's rhyme and folk song is a sign of originality'. In contrast to jargon as denaturalised language, dialect represents an independent language organism. Of course one must at the same time guard against romantic regression. Neither the postilion's horn in the forest nor the merry peasant can be offered to today's children as valid images. The excavation of what is original and timeless in traditional texts is again left to the intellectual and didactic capacity of the teacher. The 'Notes and Instructions' at the back of the five Orff-Schulwerk volumes, that are far too seldom noticed, can be of significant help when making deliberations of this kind.

Work with Schulwerk takes the form of teaching groups. This has not arisen from a shortage of teachers or of time, but corresponds rather to the nature of elemental music making. Of course concurrent, individual practice remains indispensable to the mastery of the elementary teaching material and its techniques.

The fact that the first exercises in the realm of the pentatonic scale start with the two-note call, which, followed by three-note melodies is built upon until the semitone-free pentatonic scale is reached, no longer requires any justification today. Even if the objection to the primary significance of the pentatonic in our musical consciousness were justified, the early work with children in the pentatonic scale would recommend itself in order to neutralise the over powerful dominance of major/minor tonality, and thereby again to set free the consciousness of modal tonality and also of the musical language of our century. For all work in elemental music can only justify itself as an effective, preliminary study that leads to the understanding of great music in its entirety. It is especially the work in an elemental style that opens the way to *all* kinds of style. Even children who will later not practise music any more, should, through this elemental experience achieve the aim of training their critical consciousness, as stated by Aristotle (*Politics*, 8): 'One should practise music in one's youth, but in one's riper years abandon it and content oneself with the capacities acquired in youth, namely the ability to value beauty and to enjoy it in the right way.'

Gunild Keetman, as co-author of Orff-Schulwerk and through a lifelong experience of its principles and their practical realisation in music education,

* The English equivalent (from which nearly all the rhymes in this translation have been taken) would be *The Nursery Rhymes of England* (1842) and *Popular Rhymes and Nursery Tales* (1849), both collections made by James Orchard Halliwell. (M. M.)

12

has the authority to write this book that is second to none. It could be described as both preface and preparation for the first volume of *Music for Children* and for an acquaintance with the whole work. The setting down of countless experiments and practical exercises, that have grown out of an ever-renewed delight in intellectual adventure in the field of education, presents itself not only as a personal documentation, but as an immediate, realisable and practical guide for the teacher.

The author gives suggestions and examples without insisting dogmatically on one exclusive method. She offers well-tried solutions without excluding other possibilities and individual variations. Such freedom is contained in the character of Orff-Schulwerk, which is based upon models. For working with Schulwerk does not entail the study and performance of melodies and songs with ready-made accompaniments, but rather a continuous *ars inveniendi*, a spontaneous art of discovery with a hundred ways and a thousand possible structures. The main precept, of course, is that the basic artistic integrity be maintained, as much in the preliminary study and the practical and technical details as in the quality of the material used for practice.

An introduction to Orff-Schulwerk would not be complete without a presentation of elementary movement training. Here, therefore, for the first time, the attempt has been made to include co-ordinated movement exercises from the very beginning, and to take this movement training, that has not so far been written down, beyond the absolute beginning stages and to handle it in more detail.

Theory and practice of voice production, speech training and singing are, on the other hand, intentionally avoided. These subjects need a separate, specialised, expert exploitation of the material for the integration of speech, music and movement, that is offered to such an abundant degree in Orff-Schulwerk.

This book has fulfilled its intention if it can serve as a guide that will accompany the teacher's first steps into the varied landscape of Orff-Schulwerk, that will prevent him from taking the wrong track and that will show him the well-tried paths that lead to his destination.

Werner Thomas

13

Translator's Note

The English version of this book is a faithful translation of the original German text. Though the reader will realise that some passages refer to German conditions, all the material presented in the book can be applied— if not always literally—to the English way of teaching.

Where German rhymes and texts were used in the original, these have been replaced by equivalent English ones; every one of these has been discussed with and approved by the author.

In order to be consistent, I have used the English terminology in technical matters. In my experience, the American and Canadian readers are as familiar with the English terms, as the English are with those in use in the American Continent.

M.M.

Part One   Rhythmic-Melodic Exercises

Fundamentals

The smallest rhythmic units in two-four time are derived from children's rhymes, songs and names. They can be formed from crotchets, quavers and minims, without up-beat. These will form our 'rhythmic building bricks'.

In a similar way 'rhythmic building bricks' in three-four time can be found:

The patterns in two-four time form the rhythmic foundation for the first stages of teaching. With them the children accompany the teacher's melodies and their own playing and singing, and they play and improvise with them in many different forms.

When playing for the first time on instruments—barred instruments such as xylophone, glockenspiel and metallophone—these patterns are also used as simple accompaniment figures in the form of fifths and octaves based upon the root note C. From the drone-type[1] accompaniments, moving drone and other forms of ostinato[2] accompaniment are developed.

The first melodies on barred instruments—they are played and sung—start with the cuckoo-call (see the first songs in Orff-Schulwerk) and, with a gradually increasing note range they prepare for the conscious listening to, playing by ear and writing down of the different intervals and degrees of the scale. By way of a three and then a four note range the semitone-free pentatonic scale, built upon C, is reached, completed through the upper octave repetition and retained for a long time:

In this same note range progressive attempts at discovering their own melodies are made.

[1] The term 'drone' originally referred to open strings that sounded continuously (Hurdy-gurdy) or wind pipes (Bagpipes) that were based upon the key note together with fifth or octave. 'Moving drone' accompaniments include neighbouring notes (see notation example under 'Making up accompaniments' in the chapter 'Melodic Exercises' p. 88 ff. and Orff-Schulwerk, *Music for Children*, Vol. I, pp. 82–85, Schott, London, 1958).

[2] Ostinato = obstinate
Ostinato or ostinato accompaniment = an accompanying figure that repeats itself continuously without alteration.

'In this realm (the pentatonic scale) that corresponds to his mentality the child can most easily find individual possibilities for expression, without being exposed to the danger of leaning upon the over strong examples of other music.' (C.O.)

A further advantage of making music in the pentatonic scale is the absence of semi-tones, that makes it possible to play together in an ensemble that is always free from dissonance. The imitation of melodies on barred instruments can follow in another way—apart from that already suggested that pre-supposes the conscious hearing of intervals—that is at first easier for the child. In melodies that are constructed from ascending or descending parts of the pentatonic scale it is not a question of hearing individual intervals, but rather the comprehending of a rising or falling flow of movement in which all the notes of the pentatonic scale, including the upper octaves, can soon be used (see 'Pieces and songs using scale sections' from *Melodic Exercises*, p. 70 ff.).

All good children's songs that correspond to the range of a young child's voice can be used as song material whether they are in pentatonic, major or minor keys.

Out of the 'rhythmic building bricks', through placing them side by side, separate forms are made, the shortest possible consisting of two phrases each not longer than two two-four bars, such as are found in children's rhymes:

By adding a new part of the same length a two-part binary AB form results:

A final repetition of the A part leads to a ternary ABA form, and the addition of further episodes like B above leads to rondo form ABACA etc.

18

The episodes should provide a rhythmic contrast to the main part and should lead back to it; in doing so they can either be complete in themselves, or they can, as in C below, provide a connecting link that leads back to the A part: ↳ unresolved 8ᵗʰ notes

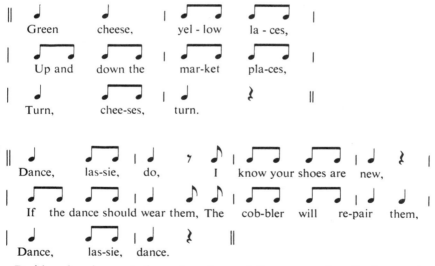

Exceptions to the usual symmetrical forms (shortenings or extensions) can easily be understood by children through using corresponding texts:

Green cheese, yel-low la-ces,

Up and down the mar-ket pla-ces,

Turn, chee-ses, turn.

Dance, las-sie, do, I know your shoes are new,

If the dance should wear them, The cob-bler will re-pair them,

Dance, las-sie, dance.

Besides clapping, patschen, stamping and finger-snapping, further modes of expression in elemental body-sounds are to be found in speaking, calling and singing. Extended and complemented by the playing of rhythm and melody instruments, they provide a comprehensive musical foundation for the child.

19

Clapping, patschen, stamping and finger-snapping are described in the following summary as 'sound gestures'; they require a detailed description.

Clapping (*Cl.*) Good clapping requires an upright but not stiff posture and enough space to move the arms freely, so the children should not be too close to one another. The fingers of one hand, lightly tensioned, strike with a rebound upon the other hand that is held like a plate. The extent of movement is in proportion to the speed: large continuous movement in a slow tempo; small movements coming more from the wrist in a fast tempo. Clapping is usually carried out in front of the body at waist height, but as a variation it can occur behind the body, above the head, or to the side.

Sound variations: loud and soft clapping, the hollow sound of clapping with cupped hands, or the whip-like sound of a few fingers on the base of the palm. Notation:

Cl.

Patschen (*Pa.*) Sometimes described as knee-slapping this denotes a flat-handed slap with rebound on the thigh near to the knee. It requires a relaxed posture and can be executed when standing with feet slightly apart, or when sitting. Patschen can be carried out as follows:

1. Both hands simultaneously—notation: upward stems throughout.

Pa.

2. As a single slap with right or left hand—notation: right hand, stems upwards; left hand, stems downwards.

Pa.

3. As a combination of hands together and separately—notation: hands together, stems upwards *and* downwards.

Pa.

4. Crossed over (right hand slaps left knee and vice versa)—notation: two lines close together, the upper line represents the right knee, the lower the left.

Stamping (*St.*) This is the accentuated placing on the floor of the sole of one foot next to the other. The starting position in a slow tempo (particularly in combination with clapping or patschen) is standing, knees side by side and slightly bent. As the foot strikes the floor the knees straighten.

Preparatory practice: Standing with feet together, bend and stretch the knees with the accent on the stretch.

In a fast tempo the accented bending and stretching are omitted. Stamping can be carried out with one foot only, or with both feet alternating, when it can lead to locomotion away from one spot. Notation: right foot, stems upwards; left foot stems downwards.

Stamping that is too heavy, particularly with bare feet, is to be avoided.

Snapping (*Sn.*) The thumb and middle or ring finger can together produce a new sound quality. Depending on the tempo it can be done with or without a supporting arm thrust, in all directions, with both hands together, with one hand continuously, or alternately with right and left hand. Notation: both hands together, upward stems throughout; hands alternately, right hand— upward stems, left hand—downward stems.

All sound gestures are practised individually and later combined together, the simplest combination to begin with being clapping and patschen.

Notation for all sound gestures combined:

In play with sound gestures one can see the beginnings of a movement orientated, elemental music making.

Advice on good and correct calling, speaking and singing do not belong within the framework of this presentation. Nevertheless, the many different kinds of speech work and songs in Schulwerk demand continuous work on the part of the teacher to perfect his knowledge of vocal techniques and dramatic presentation. Voice production and training are therefore necessary for achieving success.

Instruments to be used in the early stages

Percussion instruments: Hardwood or bamboo sticks (claves), rattles, sleigh bells, coconut shells, castanets, woodblocks, tubular woodblocks, triangle, large cymbals, small cymbals, finger cymbals, bongos, tambours, tambourines, bass drum, timpani.

Melody instruments: xylophones, glockenspiels, metallophones, tuned glasses, recorders, violoncello, viola da gamba or bordun,* guitar or lute.

Instructions on the playing technique of these instruments can be found in the Appendix.

*A two-stringed, drone bass instrument.

Rhythmic Exercises

Disposition and posture

When practising, exercises with sound gestures an arrangement must be chosen that will allow every child to see the teacher easily, and that will give him sufficient space to move his arms freely.

Possible suitable arrangements: free distribution throughout the room, each child with sufficient space of his own, or a wide semi-circle at sufficient distance from the teacher. A circle is not a suitable formation for practising ✳ sound gestures where the children are copying the teacher mirror-wise.

Exercises with sound gestures can be carried out standing or seated; as a variation they can also be done when kneeling or sitting on the floor.

For sitting, flat stools or small, cube-shaped, wooden stage blocks (that can also be used as sound producers) are suitable. With the thighs in a horizontal position the feet should be able to reach the floor easily; the posture should be upright with the upper part of the body and the arms free from tension. The sitting position should not be too comfortable (ready to spring to the feet) and should be forward on the front edge of stool or cube. To establish and confirm the idea of a good posture one should let the children, at the beginning of the lesson, alternate between an upright posture and a slovenly, round-shouldered one.

✳ Reaction training

Ability to react is a fundamental prerequisite for making music together; reaction exercises should therefore have a large share in the teaching, particularly in the early stages. The following exercises are thought of in terms of clapping, but other sound gestures can also be used.

Exercises

1. Starting together: From an 'at ease' position with the arms raised forwards at shoulder height, elbows slightly bent, either seated or standing, the first beat follows from a slight lift of the arms that is supported by an intake of breath (preparatory movement for conducting). At first only one beat or clap is asked for and this initial beat is repeated often, but at irregular intervals. Then a succession of claps is asked for for a short length of time. *this can* This is also repeated, always in a different tempo that must be recognisable *✳ also be seen in* through the teacher's preparatory movement. At first the teacher claps with *the seated* the children, then he just conducts the respective initial entries. *introduction to mallet*

2. Clapping together: This should be buoyant and full-sounding, in equal *technique* note values and without accent. The children must adapt themselves to the *when they* teacher with regard to: *are played on the floor*
—gradual changes of volume of sound in a steady tempo, *(this whole sequence can be used in that setting)*

23

—gradual changes of tempo with at first only slight divergence from the starting tempo, this also combined with changing volume,
—sudden changes of volume.

This can be practised: with everyone; with a change from one group to one or more other groups; or from child to child (in a predetermined order or in response to a call or glance).

Instead of conducting or clapping with the children the teacher can lead the exercise through an improvised melody that can be sung or played on an instrument.

Between times: The children clap all together as fast, as loudly, as softly, as slowly as they can. Their facial expressions should not be rigid. Posture correction and relaxation exercises should be given (see section on movement).

3. Finishing together: This is indicated by the teacher through his movements while clapping or conducting, or is similarly led by means of a melody or through response to a call.

4. Continuing and maintaining a tempo started by the teacher: A few beats are given to start with and the children continue to clap in this tempo. When repeating this exercise always take a different tempo. Control and correction should come from the children.

Sudden dynamic differences in accompanying a melody played by the teacher: clapping softly to the melody, loudly when it stops. Working out contrasts of loud and soft.

5. Finding the pulse of a melody improvised by the teacher. When repeating this exercise always establish a different tempo, and, according to the capacity of the children, also a different time signature.

Finding 'rhythmic building bricks'

'Rhythmic building bricks' can be extracted from children's rhymes or songs. The verses are first spoken and clapped in their complete form, then short, rhythmic units are used as continuous, underlying accompaniments that are spoken or clapped by another group.

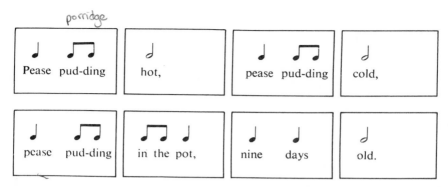

porridge

| Pease pud-ding | hot, | pease pud-ding | cold, |

| pease pud-ding | in the pot, | nine days | old. |

The individual names of children provide another source: each child speaks his own name clearly and with proper accentuation, and claps the appropriate rhythm. Names in different time-patterns, with and without up-beat, will present themselves. (The children are not made consciously aware of the various rhythmic problems that may arise.)

Variously sounding names can be clapped in the same rhythm, for instance:
John, James, Anne, Jane;
Elizabeth, Penelope, Veronica; *w/ upbeat*
Timothy, Jennifer, Christopher, etc. *opt /or with rest*   *can be used for learning irregular meter (5/8 or 7/8)*

All kinds of rhythmic games that are not difficult, and that enliven a lesson, can be developed from such material.

New names for the rhythms are found: Names of flowers, trees, bushes, animals, spices, etc.

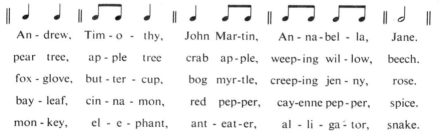

An - drew,	Tim - o - thy,	John Mar-tin,	An - na-bel - la,	Jane.
pear tree,	ap - ple tree	crab ap-ple,	weep-ing wil - low,	beech.
fox - glove,	but - ter - cup,	bog myr-tle,	creep-ing jen - ny,	rose.
bay - leaf,	cin - na - mon,	red pep-per,	cay-enne pep - per,	spice.
mon - key,	el - e - phant,	ant - eat-er,	al - li - ga - tor,	snake.

As the work progresses only those words that correspond to the selected building bricks are used. Five suitable names are chosen that are then used as symbols for the five rhythms. It is expedient at the beginning always to use the same names as models until the association of word and rhythm is quite secure.

learned / After many games and activities

This is the moment to introduce children to the notation of the rhythms that are by now familiar, and to start clapping from notation and writing rhythms in notation for themselves. The pleasure of interpreting musical notation, of holding on to a rhythm so that it can be repeated at will, of

25

writing out his own rhythms, also the pleasure in the activity of writing musical notation as such, and the ensuing visual picture; all these are incentives for children to learn to read and write in musical notation. Here too the names chosen as models can be useful.

After the foregoing exercises most children do not find it difficult to find the rhythm that corresponds to one of the model words when these rhythms are distributed over the blackboard. (The number of syllables corresponds to the number of notes.) When the teacher at first points to individual words, later to several one after the other, the children respond with the model word while one child can tap the rhythm audibly on the blackboard, underneath the written notes; at a later stage the rhythms are clapped.

When the position is reversed and the teacher claps one of the rhythms, later more than one, individual children can indicate the appropriate rhythm on the board.

Several of our rhythms are now written in one line and are reproduced by the children by means of model words or clapping. Even at this stage one should be careful to maintain a continuous, rhythmic flow, so that a new unity arises out of the shorter fragments, and that this unity is not allowed to be impaired by any written divisions such as bar lines. (use of nouses)

Memory exercises can be included: a written rhythm, after a short time being allowed for study, is rubbed off the board and the children are then asked to clap it; or a previously worked out rhythmic entity has to be repeated from memory at the end of the lesson. These are two possibilities among others.

Distinguishing between crotchets, quavers and minims and writing down these note values can be begun together with the first and earliest attempts at writing as such, even though the children do not need to know their exact meaning. in earlier stages

It is left to the teacher to decide how to set about this; nevertheless, the early stages should be concerned with large, rhythmic movement sequences related to the shapes of notation (made with a finger on the table or with a felt pen on a large sheet of paper). The laborious filling-in of the note heads that interrupts the flow should in all cases be avoided.

At a later stage, when writing in a manuscript book (the lines of the staff should be as far apart as possible, and the pen should have a soft felt nib), attention should be paid to a clean, clear result. The notes should not be written too small nor too close together; the stems should be vertical and the notes should be spaced in their correct rhythmic proportion.

The writing down of short rhythmic patterns can soon, through the notating of previously clapped rhythms (echo-play, speaking model words) extend to lengths of one, two or more bars.

Short rhymes can now also be rhythmically notated. The relevant model

26

words are found, spoken as a whole; the complete sequence is written out and the original text spoken once more, e.g.:

Rain, rain, go a - way, lit - tle John-ny wants to play.
pear tree, ap - ple tree, weep - ing wil - low, ap - ple tree.

As the work develops the model words should be less and less used, and gradually disappear altogether. At the same time exercises in beating time and conducting can be included (compare 'Leading a group, making up accompaniments, completing phrases' from *Rhythmic Exercises*, p. 53 ff.).

As for two-four time, so can names and other words provide help in the recognition and establishing of the first rhythms to be used in three-four time. In spite of their ambiguity they are helpful in the beginning stages. e.g.

Ur - su - la, Pe - ter, Ju - dy, Paul.
an - cho - vy, pil - chard, her - ring, eel.

Through repeated use in combination with their appropriate rhythms, these patterns imprint themselves quickly and are soon securely recognised and reproduced in reading and writing.

Games with 'rhythmic building bricks' —

Echo-play and other exercises

In rhythmic echo-play the teacher claps a phrase of one, two or more bars in length that is to be appropriately imitated by the children. Rhythms that are not accurately reproduced by nearly all the children are repeated.

Starting with a slow tempo, a simple structure and a firm lead from the teacher are necessary.

Echo-play trains accurate listening, quick reaction, memory and feeling for form.

Teacher
Children

T.
Chn.

27

Echo-play is later carried out while moving, in combination with walking. One should not carry on with these exercises for too long at a stretch, especially with small children, but rather repeat them often. Instead of just clapping, other sound gestures are included:

Echo-play, particularly where different sound gestures are used, should sometimes be carried out with the eyes shut.

Echo-play can be used to help the learning of a rhythmic phrase that is too long to be grasped as a whole, but that can be learnt in short sections. These short sections are played in sequence many times,

T. Cl. ‖ ♩♩♩𝅗𝅥 | − | − | ♩♩♩𝅗𝅥 | − | − | ♫♫♫ | ♩♩♩ | − | − | ♩♩𝅗𝅥 | − | − | ‖

and then clapped as a whole.

elemental

This provides an opportunity for trying out different dynamic possibilities:

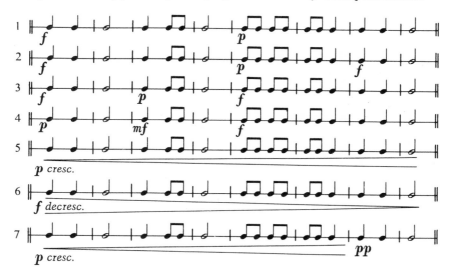

These examples can be further extended by asking the children for suggestions. Echo-play can be used at all stages of development, and patterns that include dotted rhythms, syncopation, triplets or up-beat starts are given, without at first bringing these features to conscious attention.

29

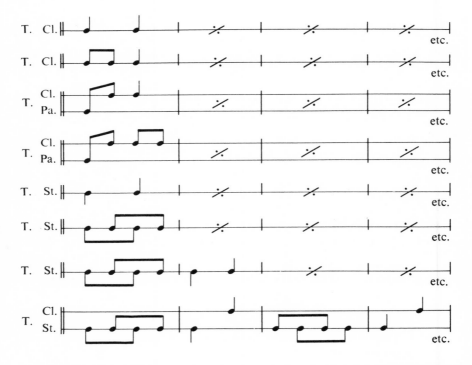

A variation of echo-play: Teacher and children begin together with a simple rhythmic phrase and after a while the teacher changes his. The children must make each change as soon as they can. The teacher changes the current rhythm only when most of the children are doing it correctly.

Other sound gestures can be used to repeat a pattern that has been clapped. This clapped rhythm

can be repeated as follows:

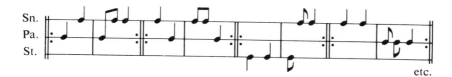

etc.

Another possibility for this kind of echo-play (the teacher claps and individual children take it in turns to provide the imitative response):

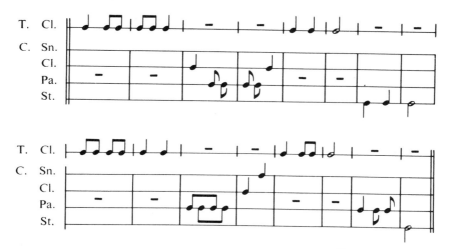

Independent forms can be made from sound gestures. They must have a simple and organic structure so that the children can remember them easily. A thorough knowledge of the structure as a whole will lead to a lively and dynamic presentation, and this is a prerequisite for a convincing performance.

Schröder
Level II
Day 1
elemental form
exercise

31

A freely improvised response to a phrase given by the teacher provides relief from the exact repetition of rhythmic patterns in the various echo games. (See 'Leading a group, making up accompaniments, completing phrases' from *Rhythmic Exercises*, p. 53 ff.)

Another game: The five 'building brick' rhythms in two-four time are divided amongst five groups standing spread out in different parts of the room:

The teacher gives a sign to one group who continue to clap their rhythm until the sign is given to another group. After several repetitions of the same sequence the children repeat it without the teacher's help. At first the changes from one group to another should not be quick. They can increase in speed later. Here too the form must be clear, for instance:

The rhythms can also be produced with sound gestures or percussion instruments; in doing so the matching of instrument and rhythm should be borne in mind: instruments with a long reverberation time for longer note values, shorter reverberation time for shorter note values. The teacher lets the children discover the possibilities.

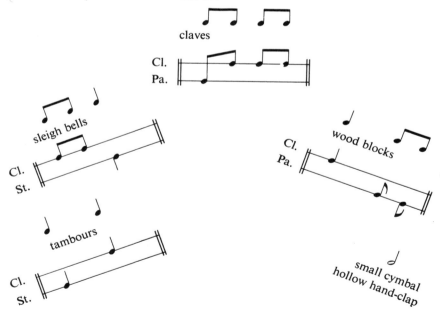

Developing from the previous examples where only one ostinato at a time was used, we can now use two and more ostinati simultaneously. Two groups enter one after the other with different ostinato accompaniment patterns, e.g.

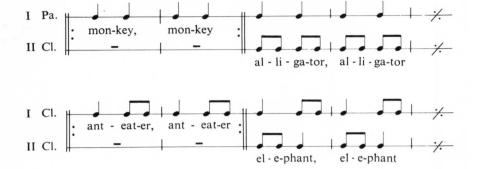

The teacher improvises a melody to this accompaniment.

✳ The same idea using different sound gestures:

Several ostinati (with sound gestures or percussion instruments) are played simultaneously, entering one after the other:

Rec.

Sn. (Tam.)

Cl. (Wb.)

Pa. (Mar.)

St. (B.D.)

etc.

etc.

It is only a small step from playing several ostinati in different groups to the *the students can independently play and listen at the same time* formation of the first canons. The following provide possibilities using two-bar rhythm patterns:

Through the use of sound gestures the canon is also seen:

Sn.
Cl.
Pa.
St.

Technique of presentation: The children start to clap one of these rhythms; after a while the teacher joins them, but in canon, and the children must not allow themselves to be put off; they should be able to hear what the teacher is doing. Next time the teacher starts and individual children (later groups) must try to find the correct moment for the canonic entry. In the end two groups that are facing one another perform the canon to which the teacher improvises a melody.

The canonic entries can come after a predetermined time (after the pattern has occurred twice for instance) or as soon as possible. Begin in a slow tempo.

The two-bar canon type ostinati can later be extended into longer forms, e.g.:

Sn.
Cl.
Pa.
St.

35

Another kind of canon for the more advanced develops from echo-play, and is improvised by the teacher. He gradually fills up the empty bar that had previously been left for the echo, and the children, while they are making this echo, must at the same time be taking in the next rhythmic pattern.

The teacher must develop and prepare the transition from echo-play to canon and facilitate the taking in of the canon through using clear structure, a succession of rhythmic patterns that are clearly distinguishable from one another and varied levels of volume. Occasional repetition of the same rhythmic pattern over several bars conceals the canon and makes it possible, when necessary, for everyone to find themselves again, e.g.:

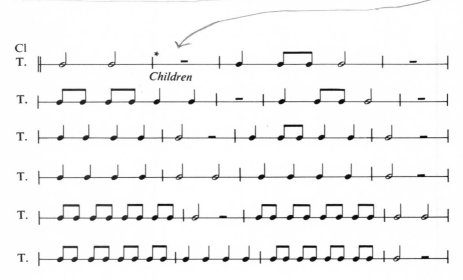

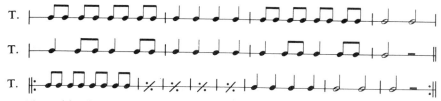

Alongside the practice of improvised canons the playing of canons that have been previously worked out should not be neglected.* Through dividing the parts between instruments of different pitch (high and low pitched drums) or between instruments of different types (drums and claves, or wood blocks and tambourines) the two parts are made clearly distinguishable.

Through the use of different sound gestures the following of the one part by the other is also made visibly clear. Another way of making the canon visible is through the connection with movement (cf. *Movement Pieces*, p. 155 ff.).

Accompaniments to given melodies

The 'rhythmic building bricks' are used in different ways as ostinato accompaniments. They can be clapped or transferred to other sound gestures or to percussion instruments.

---

* Examples of rhythmic canons are to be found in Orff-Schulwerk, *Music for Children*, Vol. I. Schott, London, pp. 74/75.

At first the children give an accompaniment pattern by themselves (rhythmic security and independence can be tested by getting them, while making the sound gestures, to answer the teacher's verbal questions without interrupting the flow of the rhythm). At a later stage, when playing a melody over such an accompaniment, the subordinate and accommodating role of the accompaniment can be practised through making slight variations in tempo and dynamics in the melody, that must immediately be taken up in the accompaniment.

Possibilities for variation

Two groups with different accompaniment rhythms alternate in accompanying the teacher's melody; working with from four to eight bar phrases the groups react at first to a sign from the teacher, then later they must themselves hear when to come in and when to stop.

Or:

Two groups with different rhythms play simultaneously as an accompaniment to the teacher's melody and exchange rhythms at a sign from the teacher.

Or:

The accompaniment is distributed between two soloists or between two instrumental groups:

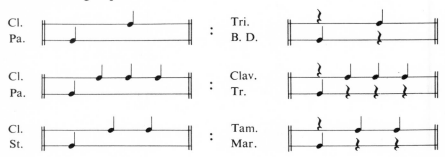

Or:

While the teacher plays a melody to an accompaniment provided by some of the children another group moves about the room, walking in two-four or three-four time, running, skipping or galloping:

40

Accompanying one's own speaking and singing

Every child, from its youngest years, gets to know rhymes and sayings that it soon picks up from adults. Pleasure in the consonance of the rhyme, in the speech rhythm and in the awakening of the imagination are often as determining for this as the interest in speaking itself, in articulation, in the rise and fall of the pitch of the speaking voice, in loud and soft speech, in whispering, and also in the intoning of the counting out rhyme. Rhythmic speech plays an important part in this approach and makes use of this interest. Old rhymes and counting out verses are used and these often make an unforgettable impression on a child. It is therefore of the greatest importance to set a standard of quality in the selection of texts.

Attention must be paid to well-rounded, meaningful, clear speech, spoken naturally and at a moderate degree of loudness; thoughtless, monotonous intoning is to be avoided from the start. Speech should always have life and movement and should be supported by the breath.

An accompaniment to one's own speech or singing can follow in various forms: it can run parallel, accentuating or complementing in direct relationship to the text, or it can take the form of an underlying ostinato rhythm. The various possibilities are shown in the following examples.

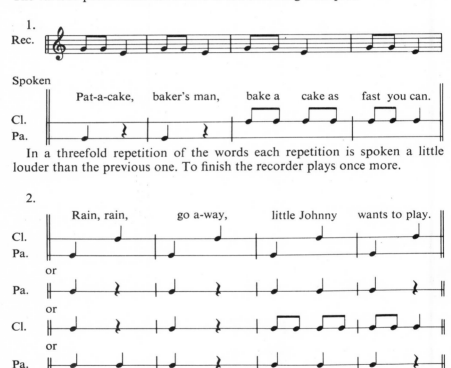

In a threefold repetition of the words each repetition is spoken a little louder than the previous one. To finish the recorder plays once more.

Ending:

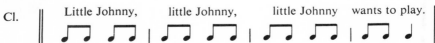

42

The individual accompaniments can first be practised alone, and several then arranged together into a sequence (individual groups one after the other or all the children together).

3.

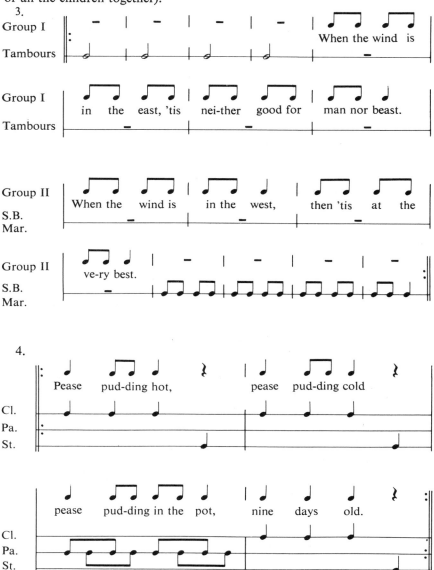

43

5.

One, two, three, four, five, once I caught a fish a-live.

Cl.
Pa.

Cl.

Tr.
Wb.

Cl.
St.

Tam.
Tr.

*Two children, facing one another, clap each other's hands.

6a)
Tri.

Come, but - ter, come, come, but - ter,

Pa.

come. Pe - ter stands at the gate,

Pa.

wait-ing for a but - ter cake, but-ter, but-ter,

Cl.
Pa.
St.

44

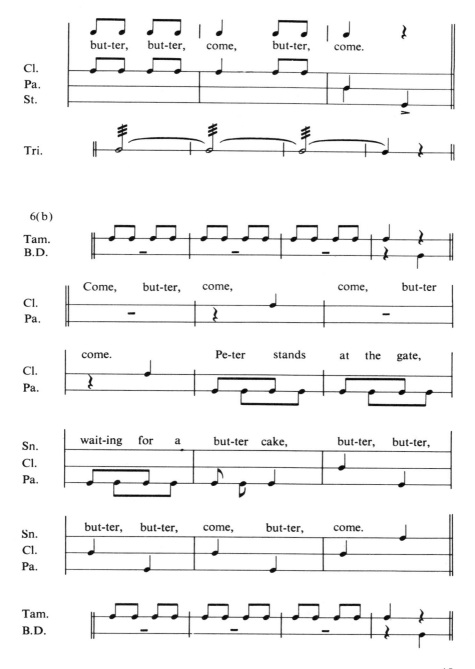

45

7.

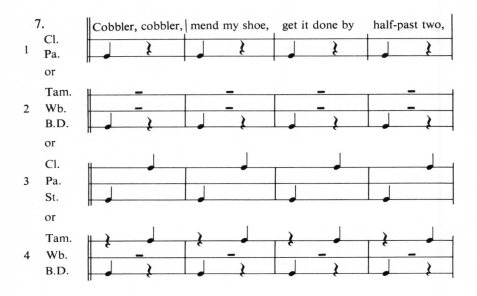

46

8.

Cuck-oo,   cher-ry tree,   catch a bird,   give it me

let the tree be high or low,   let it rain,   hail or snow.

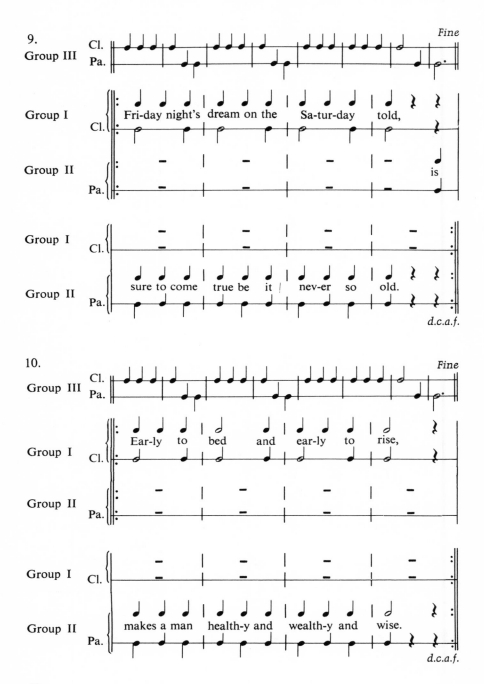

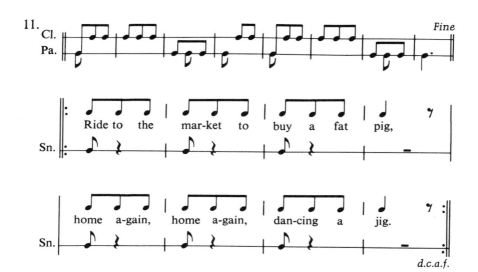

11. Cl. Pa. *Fine*

Ride to the mar-ket to buy a fat pig,

home a-gain, home a-gain, dan-cing a jig.

d.c.a.f.

12.

As round as an ap-ple as deep as a cup, and all the King's horses can't pull it up. As up.

13.

If one wants to bring together texts such as the last three into a larger form, one can link them with a refrain-like episode. In such a case the texts are best spoken unaccompanied, or sung to melodies that are available or made up by the children. The following could form a possible refrain:

Suitable texts can be accompanied by onomatopoeic sounds:

a) Spoken

Tack-y tack-y tack-y | tack-y tack-y tack-y | tack-y tack-y tack-y | tum tum tum : tum.

The mil-ler he | lived on the | riv-er of | Dee, and

no one was | sing-ing so | mer-ri-ly as | he.

d.c.a.f.

b)

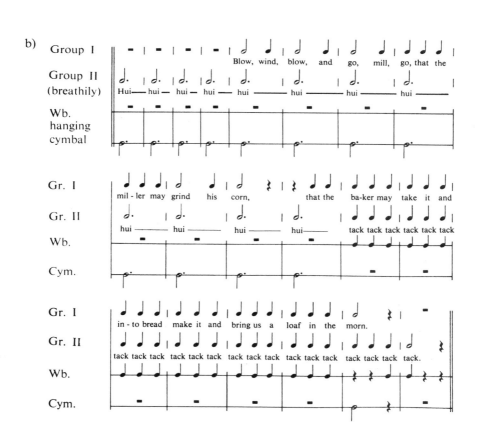

Group I — Blow, wind, blow, and go, mill, go, that the

Group II (breathily) — Hui— hui — hui — hui — hui — hui — hui —

Wb.
hanging
cymbal

Gr. I — mil-ler may grind his corn, that the ba-ker may take it and

Gr. II — hui — hui — hui — hui — tack tack tack tack tack tack

Wb.

Cym.

Gr. I — in-to bread make it and bring us a loaf in the morn.

Gr. II — tack tack tack tack tack tack tack tack tack tack tack tack tack tack tack tack.

Wb.

Cym.

51

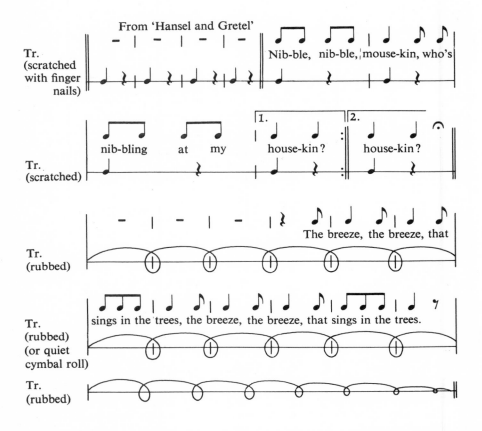

From 'Hansel and Gretel'

Tr. (scratched with finger nails)

Nib-ble, nib-ble, mouse-kin, who's

nib-bling at my house-kin? house-kin?

Tr. (scratched)

The breeze, the breeze, that

Tr. (rubbed)

sings in the trees, the breeze, the breeze, that sings in the trees.

Tr. (rubbed) (or quiet cymbal roll)

Tr. (rubbed)

In the last example tambours are scratched with the fingernails in short, precise strokes; in the second part the flat palm of the hand sweeps over the skin in the rhythm of the speech.

Possible variations in performing the texts:
—alternation between tutti, groups and soloists,
—alternation between girls and boys,
—alternation between light and dark voices,
—alternation between accompanied and unaccompanied speech,
—variations of tempo and dynamics, where appropriate.

Song texts that give inducement to particular forms of action or play can be accompanied by the appropriate gestures in rhythmic form. Songs about baking bread or cakes can be accompanied by movements that suggest stirring the dough, rolling it, kneading it and shaping it; or songs like 'Shoe

52

the little horse' lend themselves to accompaniments that imitate the trotting
sound of horses' hooves through a simple clap-patsch rhythm:

or through striking coconut shells one against the other.

Texts to which accompaniments can be invented:

> Rain on the green grass and rain on the tree,
> Rain on the house-top, but not on me.

> Cataline and Cato, Pericles and Plato,
> All they could eat was cold boiled potato.

> Round and round the rugged rock the ragged rascal ran.

> Jack Sprat could eat no fat, his wife could eat no lean,
> And so between them both, you see, they licked the platter clean.

> Diddlety, diddlety, dumpty, the cat ran up the plum tree,
> Half a crown to fetch her down, diddlety, diddlety, dumpty.

Leading a group, making up accompaniments, completing phrases

Already at an early stage children should be accustomed, on every occasion,
to take responsibility for leading a group. Opportunities for doing this occur
in reaction exercises in which the child takes the place of the teacher, for
instance in *clapping together:*
—giving the indications for starting and finishing,
—when maintaining a given tempo,
—when varying the dynamics (in a maintained tempo),
—when varying the tempo, and so on.

These exercises can also be tried for giving practice in beating time or
conducting.

Beating time relates to the actions needed for giving tempo and barring.

Conducting presupposes the ability to beat time, but goes further in imply-
ing ability to lead a group, and to shape a piece of music. Entries, structure
and endings must be indicated through gesture; the whole musical flow must
be controlled. Only the initial stages of this responsible task can be realised by
the child, but appropriate attempts should continue to be made from time to
time. Speaking or singing with the other children helps to make it easier.

In the making up of new patterns and in exercises for completing phrases (question and answer) the children work with the material already learnt independently and freely, and new variations are practised at every stage. Imagination and a feeling for form are needed for this and these will be awakened and encouraged by these exercises.

First exercises can comprise:

finding new words to given rhythms,

later:

—making up clapped ostinato patterns,
—transferring clapped accompaniments to other sound gestures or percussion instruments,
—inventing accompaniments using sound gestures or percussion instruments,
—inventing accompaniments to spoken texts,
—inventing texts and rhymes to rhythmic phrases, and so on.

In rhythmic question and answer exercises, developed from echo-play, a rhythmic phrase initiated by the teacher must be freely carried further by a child. The aim is that the two parts, in form and content, should constitute a unity. Formal unity can be achieved (at first) through equal length, unity of content (when the phrases are not too short) through the use of material contained in the first part of the question, and also through contrasted sections. Most children react unconsciously and show a feeling for form; they should always be made to recognise, however, through the help of the teacher and through their own observation, which solutions were good, and why, and the reverse.

Rhythmic question and answer games, as for echo-play, are maintained in a continuous exchange between the teacher and individual children. It is important that the answers should start at the right time and convincingly, and that there should be an uninterrupted flow as each new person takes over. As far as possible children should not be allowed to correct themselves. A neutral accompaniment helps to maintain the continuity. According to the capacity of the children the teacher will begin with two- or four-bar phrases in two-four time, later also in other time signatures. With increasing security in terms of form an uneven number of bars can be used, or some of the answering phrases can be longer or shorter than that given by the teacher.

Various possibilities for rhythmic question and answer

The teacher gives the same question several times; each child answers differently:

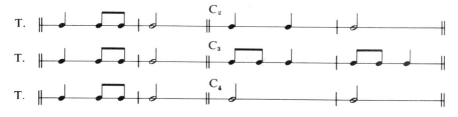

Or:

The teacher always gives a different question:

Or:

To make the formal relationship between the two halves clear the children must repeat either the opening or the final bars in their answer:

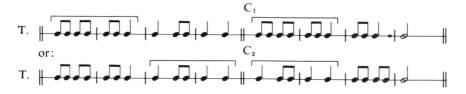

Or:

A child takes the teacher's place in echo-play and in the interchange between him and the others he must always think of new rhythms. In this instance the following are important: clear recognisable form, uninterrupted flow, a wealth of variety, and careful observation of the rest of the class so that he can react quickly and repeat a phrase that was not returned accurately.

Or:

Two children have a rhythmic 'conversation' with one another either clapping or on percussion instruments, with a constant exchange of question and answer.

Or:

A child invents both the opening *and* the answering phrase of a rhythm:

This can be learnt by all the children, and, using suggestions from the children it can be transferred to sound gestures, for example:

With the addition of the following improvised episodes (B, C, etc.)

that alternate with the first rhythm, a rondo is made with the parts A (first rhythm) BACA.

In a possible further development—it includes the use of barred percussion that, though described in the later chapter on melodic exercises, should by now have been in practice for some time—the following could be the next task:

Invent a melody for soprano xylophone to the rhythm of the A part, and add to this an ostinato accompaniment for alto xylophone and other simple percussion instruments.

A possible arrangement would be:

56

This section can also be used as an A theme for a rondo.

Solo improvisations—on bass drum, tambourine, claves, small cymbals and similar instruments—can form the episodes. A collectively discovered movement form, the easiest being that based on the form of a circle, completes the development.

Examples in other time-signatures can be worked out in the same way. Again a rhythm, taken from a question and answer or invented by one child alone, is used as a basis,

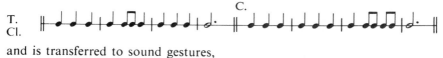

and is transferred to sound gestures,

is then further melodically transferred to barred instruments and filled out instrumentally,

and through improvised episodes of the same length turned into a rondo.

Here is an example of an ABA form in six-eight time structured in the same way:

Another improvisation task, the free rhythmic accompaniment on a chosen instrument (drum, tambourine, claves, etc.) of a melody that can be either known or improvised by the teacher, demands adjustment to its form and style. Rhythmic parallels are to be avoided; moments of rest in the melody should, when possible, be filled out; nevertheless the independence of the whole must be preserved.

For example:

Melodic Exercises

Barred percussion instruments (xylophones, glockenspiels, metallophones) are the fundamental melodic instruments for the first stages of teaching. In order to achieve a satisfying sound when playing with larger groups the following numbers of instruments should gradually be acquired: Two or three alto and soprano xylophones, two alto and soprano glockenspiels, one alto and soprano metallophone and one bass xylophone (also useful as a substitute for timpani). The main body of sound is provided by the xylophones, brilliance and high resonance by the glockenspiels, swinging and sustained bell-like sounds by the metallophones.

For technical practice, especially of faster passages, metallophones without damping devices, because of their long reverberation time and the resulting blurred sounds, are not suitable.

Disposition and posture when playing barred percussion instruments

The arrangement of the instruments is dependent upon the available space, the number of instruments or instrumental groups and the purpose of the exercise; it will therefore often vary. In every case they should be clearly distributed and functional; those playing related groups of instruments should, where possible, stand or sit together.

For practice purposes the most convenient arrangement is to have all the instruments in a flat-shaped semi-circle, but where there are large numbers the lower pitched instruments should be in two rows, those in the back row placing their instruments between the gaps in the front row. The arrangement from right to left (from the teacher's standpoint) should be: bass xylophone, alto xylophones, soprano xylophones, alto metallophone, soprano metallophone, alto glockenspiels and soprano glockenspiels.

It is possible to arrange the instruments in blocks, either facing the teacher or opposite to one another (for instance when playing antiphonally) and also, when the room allows it, to make a circular arrangement. Timpani and the usual small percussion are placed wherever convenient.

The barred instruments should each stand on an appropriate table or other suitable surface. The height of the playing surface of the bars should be just higher than the knees of a seated child; when standing (practical with small children) correspondingly higher. The room to the side of each instrument should be sufficient to allow the child to walk easily round his instrument should this become part of an eventual movement exercise.

Posture for playing: upright, yet not rigid but relaxed, with the body leaning slightly forward and with the arms held slightly away from the sides. The distance from the instrument is such that it can easily be reached without losing a good posture. The sitting position should be on the edge of stool or chair, feet on the floor. When standing the best position is with one foot

60

slightly in front of the other, and with the weight on the front foot and more on the ball of the foot than on the heel.

The beaters are held in such a way that the end of the handle is visible; the palms face downwards and the elbows should not be pressed into the sides. The thumb holds from below, the index and middle finger hold the handle by curving gently round it—the first finger should not lie along the handle—the remaining two fingers are placed lightly on the handle. The sound is made through an elastic vertical striking action. The extent of the up-and-down movement of the beaters should not exceed the shape made by the sides of an acute angle, the extent and speed of the arm movement being relative to the speed of the notes to be played.

First exercises

The teacher plays and names the individual instruments and allows the children to establish the size, structure, material, character of sound, length of sound and difference of pitch. The children should also be able to tell with their eyes shut from which type of instrument a sound proceeds and also from which instrument. The children play a few individual notes quietly (how to play with and hold the beaters has already been explained). They play all together, one at a time, with one hand, with the other hand, with both hands together. They glide quietly from the low-pitched (dark) notes to the high-pitched (bright) ones and vice versa. They can do this all together, in groups of the same type of instruments together, the same instruments together, or individually. Individual children play short, spontaneously discovered note sequences.

After the free testing of the tone quality of the individual instruments comes the search for predetermined notes, at first the low and high C that are marked with a white spot on the xylophones (on the other instruments the position of the Cs has to be discovered through the arrangement of the notes).

The low C is played with a buoyant action of the left hand with the beater striking the middle of the bar: by individual children, then all together. By listening to one another the irregular sounds can find a common tempo at a quiet speed. Repeat this with the right hand on the top C and then with both hands together.

Play louder—never so loud that it clatters—play quieter. Always develop all quality of sound from soft playing; play without always looking at the instrument; while playing with good, upright posture look up from time to time towards the teacher, any wrong notes being heard and corrected as soon as possible.

Between whiles: loosening of arms, hands and shoulders, twisting and turning, stretching.

Starting together: lay the beater (or beaters) on the middle of the note to be played, look at the teacher, then, as he makes the preparatory movement with an intake of breath at the same time lift the beater a little, then, looking again at the instrument play the note at the required level of intensity. At first the teacher plays with the children, and then he brings them in by conducting.

Practise bringing them in several times in succession with one sound only, and at irregular intervals and at changing dynamic levels. (Tempo and dynamics are indicated by the preparatory movement of the teacher.) Next give several continuous beats at a steady tempo. Try also playing so that every alternate beat is indicated by a silent gesture with the beaters in the air (minim) and then without this (crotchet). Both beaters should rebound to the same height. In the early stages of this activity appropriate patschen exercises should be used in which the children can look all the time at the teacher without playing any wrong notes.

Finishing together: this is achieved through the teacher calling out or giving a sign; this means that the children will have to look away from their instruments in order to see him.

All reaction exercises from the chapter on rhythm should be correspondingly transferred on to barred instruments.

Accompaniments, songs, pieces

Accompaniments to improvised melodies

The 'rhythmic building bricks' mentioned in the first part of this book are also fundamental to the early stages of melodic work. After suitable preparation with patschen exercises they are used as ostinato accompaniments. The different rhythms are at first played with both hands together on octaves or fifths based on C. The teacher improvises short melodies to this. Other notes are added.

The simultaneous playing of several accompaniments in the same rhythm but on different notes within the individual instrumental groups will achieve the simplest kind of tonal enrichment. In the following example such a group of ostinati is shown but in practice the players should come in one after the other at one or two bars distance.

Various possibilities when playing ostinato accompaniments to improvised melodies:

Changes of dynamics: playing softly as long as the teacher plays the melody, playing loudly (don't overdo it!) when he stops;

or: as above but alternating between two different instrumental groups who are playing the same accompaniment;

or: alternating between two instrumental groups with different accompaniments;

or: alternating between two accompaniments played by all children in the same group;

or: alternately playing an accompaniment and getting up and circling round one's instrument in whatever way is prescribed, each activity to last for the same period of time;

or: the same with two alternating groups;

or: reacting to gradual changes of tempo in the melody.

Accompanying two and three note songs

In contrast to the freely chosen accompaniments to which a melody is to be improvised, where the melody has to accommodate itself to the accompaniment, those accompaniments that are to provide a foundation to a given melody must follow certain rules. Above all, parallel movement with the melody must be avoided whenever possible. It is best at first to use neutral accompaniments (main notes: tonic or key note, fifth or octave above, with even, continuous rhythms) that can later be varied through the inclusion of other notes.

In each of the following songs several accompaniments are given, representing different grades of difficulty, from which the teacher can find one suitable for the children he teaches. Easier accompaniments can be substituted for those that are too difficult (in the previous songs as well), two-part accompaniments can be played by two children, accompaniments in which each hand has a different rhythm can be prepared through appropriate patschen exercises.

Pa.

barred
instrument

At first the teacher sings or plays the melody to the children's accompaniment, later they will sing it as they play. In the first three of the following examples where the melody appears at the higher octave it is of course only played at this pitch, the voices remain at the lower pitch. Pay attention to the soft playing of accompaniments so that the singing can come through more strongly. Which instruments should play the melody and which should accompany is left to the teacher to decide. As a rule, the soprano xylophone for the melody and the alto xylophone for the accompaniment are the most suitable. To have a change of timbre, however, glockenspiels and, if necessary, metallophones and the bass xylophone should also be brought into play.

Cuck-oo, where are you? Cuck-oo, where are you? Cuck-oo, where are you? Cuck-oo, where are you?

Further accompaniments

Rain, rain, go a-way, lit-tle John-ny wants to play. Rain, rain, go a-way, lit-tle John-ny wants to play.

Further accompaniments

Pat-a-cake, ba-ker's man, bake a cake as fast you can.

Pat-a-cake, ba-ker's man, bake a cake as fast you can.

Further accompaniments

Cuck-oo, cher-ry tree, catch a bird, give it me, let the tree be high or low, let it rain, hail or snow.

Further accompaniments

Wb.

One, two, three, four, five,   once I caught a fish a-live,

Fine

Wb.

six,   sev'n,   eight, nine, ten,   then I put it back a-gain.

	Solo 1	Solo 2
spoken	Why did you let it go?	Because it bit my finger so.

Tri.

	Solo 1	Solo 2
	Which finger did it bite?	This little finger on the right.

Tri.

d.c.a.f.

Further accompaniments

66

Further accompaniments for the first four bars

Lu-cy Locket lost her pock-et, Kit-ty Fish-er found it,

or:

not a pen-ny was there in it, just a rib-bon round it.

d.c.a.f.

Further accompaniments

Ind.

Doc-tor Foster _ went to Gloucester

2 players

in a shower of _rain. He stepped in a pud-dle right up_ to his mid-dle and

nev-er went there a-gain.

Ind.

As a preparation for the playing of two and three note melodies the rhythm of the melody can be played on one note, preferably the key note or the fifth: with each hand alone, with both hands either together in octaves or in alternation on the one note between left and right hand, at times at the lower octave or the higher octave. By this means simple forms can be constructed, e.g.

Prelude: the rhythm of the melody is played on the key note, at first at the low pitch and then at the high (forte).

Song: teacher plays melody, children play accompaniment and sing the song at the same time (piano).

Postlude: same as prelude (forte).

Rain, rain,   go   a-way,   lit-tle John-ny   wants to play.

Songs with two and three notes

The playing of song melodies can, when necessary, be made more secure by doing preliminary exercises (using patschen for certain rhythms, playing individual bars, using fragments of the melody as exercises for playing by ear). At the same time the children are made familiar, step by step, with the staff notation as far as the notes of the songs are concerned. They see the songs they are playing written in notation on the blackboard. Slight changes that the teacher may decide to make must be sung back by the children. New patterns within this three-note range are sung from notation and played on the barred instruments.

The notation of melodies presupposes security in rhythmic notation. With one-bar patterns that are played or sung to the children the rhythmic notation is first written down, and the differences of pitch are then determined. What kind of aids, if any, the teacher wishes to use are left to him to decide, also whether he starts by using only two lines of the staff, or all five. In all cases the lines should be widely spaced at the beginning.

With an increase in the tonal range the corresponding practice in singing and playing from notation, and also in writing down in notation, go hand in hand.

Pieces and songs using scale sections

Simultaneously with the first two- and three-note melodies, songs using the whole pentatonic range of the instruments can also be worked out. They are developed through playing the ascending or descending scale, or fragments of it, in notes of equal length, either played first by the teacher or described by him. At first whole sequences can be played with one hand alone—if the weaker hand is also sometimes used its clumsiness will gradually disappear— followed by alternate use of both hands and also the technique of crossing the hands, that has been encountered in previous accompaniments and songs. When crossing the hands there must be no dynamic unevenness, the change over should be audibly imperceptible. The necessary movements should be practised in exaggerated form in the air or on the floor in both directions.

When playing in this way not only are the starting and finishing notes to be grasped, but at the same time there follows the unconscious training of the ear, that establishes the relationship of the notes of the scale to one another. This procedure can be encouraged by often interspersing echo-play with sections of the scale that are varied from time to time.

The following pieces, and also the preceding exercises, can again be played first with one hand, and later with both hands in alternation.

An exercise that the children can practise together and that helps to establish the connection between the changes of pitch and the relative movement of the beaters on the instruments is to play the melody—while singing it—'in the air'. For this the horizontal plane of movement is enlarged and the teacher should easily be able to see, through the sequence of movement, whether all children are 'playing' correctly.

70

71

72

73

✳ Various ways of extending pieces:

—repeating a piece, when possible, an octave higher,
—repeating at a different dynamic level,
—playing a piece alternately as solo and tutti,
—playing a piece alternately between different instrumental groups,
—playing the same sequence of notes but in a different rhythm or with a different time signature: three-four instead of two-four time, dotted quaver rhythm instead of even quavers, etc. (with the dotted rhythm the hands 'gallop' just as the feet do—prepare this with patschen exercises),
—the inclusion of small percussion for occasional accents,
—putting together several pieces to make a small suite,
—including rhythmic interludes or episodes,
—using the pieces to accompany various movement sequences.

The following songs provide a continuation to what has already occurred in the pieces:

Donkey, donkey, do not bray, mend your pace and trot a - way. Donkey, donkey, do not bray, mend your pace trot a - way, in - deed the mar - ket's al - most done, my but - ter's melt-ing in the sun.

Rain, rain, go a-way;

Suggestions for teaching pieces and songs

As an example, the melody that the teacher invents to the rhyme

> One, two, three,
> make a pot of tea;
> put it on the table and we'll
> all have tea.

One, two, three, make a pot of tea; put it on the table and we'll all have tea.

is to be learnt by the children and played back on barred instruments.

The rhyme is first spoken in a clear rhythm, then reproduced in clapping and in patschen. The distribution between right and left hand is decided upon and is played upon one note, the note G. The first variation to this one note melody can be played by the teacher and echoed by the children, or it can be called out: 'all have tea' is played on the notes E, D, C. The next change to be made would be the opening 'one, two, three' on the same three notes. A corresponding melodic shape for the second bar could be found by the children. The last bar to be completed (bar 3) could again be played by the teacher and copied by the children.

Or:

Using the basic melodic outline of a piece that has already been worked out one can arrive at a final product through slight rhythmic or melodic modifications. The individual modifications must be listened to and reproduced by ear on the instruments:

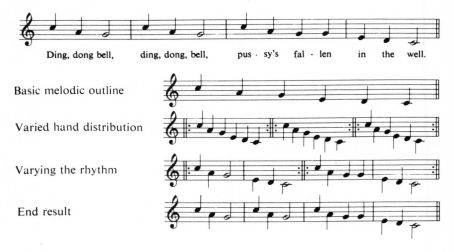

Ding, dong bell, ding, dong, bell, pus · sy's fal - len in the well.

Basic melodic outline

Varied hand distribution

Varying the rhythm

End result

With songs the teacher can first sing the whole song, then individual phrases. The children imitate by ear until they know it and can sing it alone. Striking features—the highest or lowest note—are established and named, and the entire melodic shape is drawn in the air with big movements in a continuous flow. The use of hand signs or the singing of letter names or tonic solfa syllables are possible aids.

After skilful preparation most children can play simple melodies correctly by ear at the first try. Rhythmic uncertainties can still arise, but by repeating the sequence of notes often, and by gradually increasing the speed to the natural tempo, a fluent technique can be achieved as a matter of course.

Older children who are learning suitable songs or pieces from the books can hear them several times on a gramophone record. While listening they should recognise time structure, form, instrumentation, melody and accompaniment. The main instrumental parts should be learnt by ear if possible.

Layered ostinati

While in most of the songs and pieces so far treated only one or two ostinati were played, the following examples show several ostinati placed one on top of the other to form a larger volume of sound.

Rec.

The distribution of the hands should be worked out by each individual player.

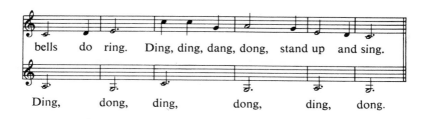

bells   do   ring.   Ding, ding, dang, dong,   stand up   and sing.

Ding,   dong,   ding,   dong,   ding,   dong.

As an exercise in playing together these 'layered ostinati' do not have to have a melody played with them as is given here in these examples. They can also be played as a type of bell ringing exercise. The teacher brings the instruments in one at a time at two-bar intervals, forming a crescendo until everyone is playing and they can then bring the piece to an end by reversing the process.

The build-up can occur from the lowest pitched instrument through to the highest or vice versa, but it can also establish other features of the structure. In the first piece, for example (p.80/81), the instruments playing ostinati with quaver movement could start, followed by those with crotchets, then minims and lastly semi-breves. The reverse order of entry is also possible but more difficult since it presupposes the ability to count the silent beats at the correct speed. The simultaneous entry of all instruments together is, of course, also possible.

The juxtaposition of a full tutti sound with that of a solo instrument, such as recorder or glockenspiel, is also attractive. To achieve thereby a successful form in the tutti a short melody can be played by several recorders in unison:

Rec.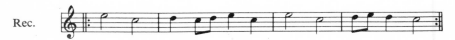

Improvising together vocally over ostinati of this kind—one voice begins, then two and more, until everyone in the various vocal ranges is joining in, all of course in the pentatonic scale—leads to an intensified sound effect and to the experience of individual contribution to a large body of sound. When attempting to build up such combined ostinati, attention should be paid to producing a good combined sound. Accompaniment forms that are rhythmically or melodically complementary provide a strong and compact support.

Making up accompaniments and completing phrases

These exercises start also with the invention of ostinato accompaniments. For the first playful experiments, attractive at every stage, we are limited here to the main notes, the octave and the fifth, later adding more notes in more free accompaniment patterns. These are tried out by the children with hands together or in alternation.

Here are some examples:

To give timid children the courage to improvise and play melodies, group improvisations, in which they do not feel so exposed, can serve as a transition to individual improvisation. Over an ostinato that provides the basic pulse for everyone the other children enter quite freely. Each child plays quietly according to his own idea of a melody; no one dominates. Carefully chosen titles such as 'Lullaby', 'By the river' or 'At the seaside' can also give a helpful stimulus in terms of mood. The individual improvisations that follow can start, as they did with the rhythmic ones, with children finishing phrases started by the teacher. These should not be too long at first.

Because most of the children do not yet have a developed sense of pitch and because rhythmic form is still difficult for them, melodies can be constructed from sections of the scale consisting mainly of notes of equal length. The rhythmic pattern given by the teacher can be repeated in the answer.

These are followed by freer versions:

<!-- margin note: Gradual increase -->

In these examples the melodies proceed by step without any large intervals, and the sound is mostly first experienced when played, but melodies containing larger intervals should also be practised and here the inner ear must hear the sound before it is played. For such melodies it is a good idea to restrict the range of sounds to be used at first, increasing this range only gradually.

To stop the melodies from becoming too breathlessly short the child can answer the teacher's phrase twice only making an ending the second time. The teacher can repeat the same questioning phrase.

A further stage would be to double the number of bars used in each section:

Melodies can end on each of the five notes; stereotype endings, particularly on the keynote C should be avoided; new solutions should always be sought.

Instead of continuing a melody started by someone else the children now improvise the beginning of the melody as well. The main idea or germ of the tune must be easily memorable so that, if necessary, it can be retained and *(and taught)* repeated. The children can now alternate with one another: one child plays the first half and a second child completes it. A neutral ostinato accompaniment that starts a few bars in advance, thus giving the improvisers time to think themselves in and to adapt to the accompaniment, stimulates the imagination and keeps the flow of the piece going. After all the preceding exercises have been experienced it is no longer difficult to improvise whole melodies that are complete in themselves. These can become the main parts or the episodes of rondos.

To build a rondo in a short time the melody for the main A part should be easy to remember and to play:

Ostinato accompaniments on barred and small percussion instruments are invented to go with this rondo A part, while the plucked open strings of a drone bass string instrument, tuned to key note and fifth above, will add some bass quality to the overall sound.

Another simple possibility for melodic improvisation lies in finding a melody to short given texts (or rhythms). A limited range of notes is also advisable here at first.

92

This exercise should also be often tried out with singing and the melodies thus invented should then be played on the instruments. At first there will be some difficulty through being limited to the notes of the pentatonic scale and this must here be consciously realised.

Side by side with improvisation in pre-structured forms the improvisation of melodies in irregular, freer phrases, that are less dependent on a metrical structure, should be attempted. Again one can begin with a kind of 'conversation' between teacher and individual children. In spite of greater freedom the connection between the individual sections must remain clear.

Still structured metrically the following examples nevertheless show uneven phrase lengths:

The following melodies are quite free from metrical structure:

Yet further melodic and rhythmic possibilities present themselves when short impromptu prose texts are sung or played on instruments:

'Are you going?' 'I'm going to bed now.' 'Sleep well, and pleas - ant dreams.'

To-mor-row we'll play in the garden if the sun comes out.'

'If it's rain-ing, we'll look out of the window.'

He who makes a detailed study of melodic improvisation will always discover new ways and forms, and these discoveries are the special attraction of the exercise.

Hints on the early stages of recorder playing

Recorder lessons should be begun as soon as possible, and of course in small groups, for much individual help is needed at first. It is important that the playing should not be stiff but flowing, and that movement should soon be included (see 'Walking with the recorder' in *Elementary Movement Training*, p. 131 f.). Side by side with the important reading from notation there should be much playing from memory right from the beginning. The songs or pieces that are learnt from memory should be used, when suitable, as movement accompaniments for other groups of children. From the beginning imitation by ear is again attempted, starting with a rhythmic sub-division of one note, via simple melodies within a small note range, within a larger note range, to phrases with rhythmic and melodic variety.

Improvisation on the recorder is developed in a similar way to that on the barred instruments: it starts with short 'conversations' between teacher and individual children—these can be metric or free—and these grow into individual forms that are soon using the whole seven note range and, with increasing skill, can include the semi-tones. Rhythmic or melodic accompaniments, episodes with sound gestures or percussion instruments, also playing the melody alternately on recorder and barred instrument, add variety to the lesson. As a buoyant support in the bass a drone on violin-cello or viola da gamba can be used.

Speech Exercises

Word series and sayings with rhythmic accompaniment

The texts collected here are different from the rhymes and songs used at the beginning because of their more varied rhythmic structure. The performance of these pieces demands a very free interpretation through changing dynamics. *Ad libitum* additional accompaniments can clarify the structure, support it rhythmically and enliven the sound. The first exercises with word series are especially suitable for stimulating visual imagery and imagination. The often asymmetrical structure is rendered as natural as child's play through the connection with words.

Some of the following pieces are extensions of examples from Orff-Schulwerk.*

Word series

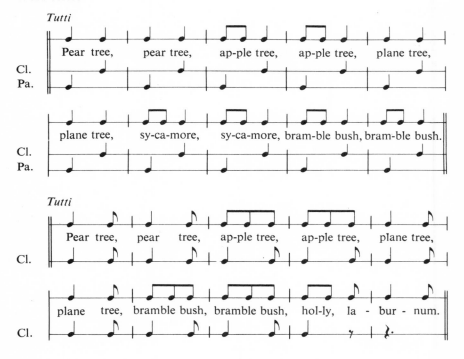

* Orff-Schulwerk, *Music for Children*, Vol. I, Schott, London, pp. 50–52.

96

bright voices, spoken very freely,

Cro-cus, nar-cis-sus, fri - til-ler - y,   pri-mu-la ver - is, jas-mine, ja - po-ni-ca.

individual voices   *Tutti*   *Solo*

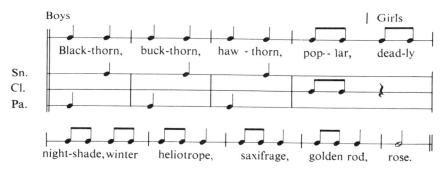

Walnut, sweet chest-nut,   magnolia, lobelia, willowherb, willowherb,   daffodil.

Triangle

Boys | Girls

Black-thorn,   buck-thorn,   haw - thorn,   pop-- lar,   dead-ly

Sn.
Cl.
Pa.

night-shade, winter   heliotrope,   saxifrage,   golden rod,   rose.

Sayings and weather lore

Gr. I   Gr. II

Sea - gull,   sea - gull,   sit   on   the   sand,   it's

Gr. I   Cl.
        Pa.

Gr. II Cl.

nev-er good   weather when   you're on the   land.

Gr. I   Cl.
        Pa.

Gr. II Cl.

Some are wise, and some are other wise.

Hanging cymbal
Triangle

Matthie, Matthie, Saint Matthie sends the sap into the tree.

Finger cymbals

Mat - thie, Mat-thie, Saint Mat - thie.

Finger cymbals

Group I   Group II
A-pril wea-ther, rain and sunshine both together.

Cl.
Pa.

Tutti
Rain and sunshine both together.

Sn.

Half a loaf is better than nothing.

Cl.
Pa.

Is better than nothing

Pa.

98

The following examples show how many proverbs (unaccompanied or accompanied) can be linked together to make longer structures. In performance the children must change quickly from one group of voices to another and from one tempo or dynamic level to another.

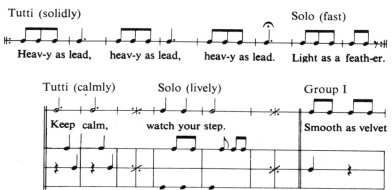

Tutti (solidly)   Solo (fast)

Heav-y as lead,   heav-y as lead,   heav-y as lead.   Light as a feath-er.

Tutti (calmly)   Solo (lively)   Group I

Keep calm,   watch your step.   Smooth as velvet

Group II   Tutti

rough as   Nothing seek,   Look before you leap
   bad-ger.   nothing find.

Proverbs that can also be spoken in canon

100

Various texts spoken together in a predetermined rhythm

Hick-up

Part Two   Elementary Movement Training

Introduction

'Elemental music is never music alone but forms a unity with movement, dance and speech.' (C. O.)

This unity, that even today is quite natural to many cultures and needs no special fostering, has, in most civilised lands been entirely lost, and only carried on in an unbroken line by children. To preserve and develop this unity for children is one of the main tasks that Orff-Schulwerk has set itself. It requires, besides the development of musical and language abilities, an elementary movement training of equal aim that is able to provide through the strong emphasis on rhythmical elements, a reciprocal benefit to musical capacity.

The present description of this training contains examples that can be used with beginners and with the more experienced. These are characterised but no specific age range is given, for age as well as ability must be taken into account in the early stages. The teacher who has some experience in movement teaching will know how to use the exercises correctly; he will also, in relation to the abundance of material, be able to select a few exercises and modify and enlarge them purposefully. The teacher who is not so conversant with material of this kind will certainly be able to incorporate the simpler exercises into his teaching, but it is nevertheless in the long run advisable, indeed necessary, for him to acquire the requisite knowledge through practical work with a professional movement teacher. In principle no Schulwerk lesson should be without movement exercises. These can at first take place in the classroom, even when space is limited, for movement can consist of 'bouncing on the spot' (the heels leave the floor returning to it with a light rebound on the pulse or whenever required), swaying the body gently to right and to left, an arm movement, an accompaniment with sound gestures (clapping, patschen, stamping, finger-snapping) or beating time to a rhythmic or melodic sequence. In the long run, however, this is not enough, and the demand for a suitable movement room (hall, gymnasium or music room) must be made. It should be sufficiently large and light, with a floor that is free from splinters and not too cold or slippery. The most ideal floor is a sprung floor that allows greater demands to be made upon the ankles. All movement work should be done in light clothes that are unrestricting, and either bare-footed or with gym shoes.

Reaction training

Reaction to acoustic or optical stimuli are among the tasks that can be undertaken in the first lesson without the prerequisite of any movement skills. This training of the senses in direct connection with physical reaction should have a large share in the early stages of teaching and should appear in every lesson in some kind of play situation.

107

The child is asked to react to an acoustic stimulus by changing the kind of movement, the direction of his travelling or the forms or groupings in which he is moving. Every child can walk, run, bounce, leap and turn on the spot more or less easily. He quickly learns to skip and gallop. The terms forwards, backwards and sideways are known to him and formations such as circle, 'freely about the room'* and 'snake formation'† will soon become well-known expressions to him, to which he learns to accommodate himself quite naturally.

The following should be undertaken: noticing when an instrumental accompaniment to the movement stops and starts again; recognising the difference in pitch between two similar instruments (two drums, woodblocks, bongos or tubular woodblocks); distinguishing between two different kinds of instrumental sounds (they can be simple percussion or barred instruments) or different accompanying rhythms. The 'rules of the game' should always be simple and clearly understandable for every child.

The following examples show some possibilities that should serve as suggestions for the teacher.

Exercises

The children walk (skip, run) in a circle (snake, freely about the room) while the teacher accompanies on a drum (on bongos or recorder). When the accompaniment stops they stand still (squat, sit down, lie down); when the accompaniment starts up again they resume their previous movement.

When they are moving freely about the room the cessation of the accompaniment could mean forming a circle with the teacher as its centre point as quickly as possible. The teacher counts slowly up to three, and by 'three' the circle must be there, with all children holding hands and equidistant from one another. To make this more difficult the teacher, while playing the accompaniment can keep changing his standing place.

Or:

The formation of the circle must be achieved in silence. At every repetition of the process the counting gets a little faster.

The alternate use of similar instruments at different pitch levels, or instruments of different types can mean: changing direction between forwards and backwards when moving freely round the room or in a circle.

---

* Walking (running or skipping) 'freely about the room' allows each child to move around the room wherever he chooses, but he must be nimble enough to avoid bumping into another child and the children should be using every part of the room equally.

† One child, the 'head' of the snake, leads the other children in snake-like paths about the room, and every twist or turn has to be followed exactly by every 'joint' in the snake's body. In order to make himself clearly visible to all the other children the 'head' may hold one arm high in the air.

108

Or:

Still travelling forwards, but in the opposite direction, while moving freely, in a circle or in snake formation (in this case the 'tail' of the snake now becomes the 'head').

Or:

Dividing the snake into two or more parts whose 'heads' are known in advance. When the first instrument comes in again the various parts join up to form one snake again.

Or:

Changing from moving freely round the room to a circular formation in pairs in a pre-arranged way, e.g. with arms around each other's waists, holding hands with hands crossed over, or with linked arms. The partner that has to be found as soon as possible can be the nearest child or always the same one. The movement is not interrupted, and the partners adapt to one another's steps.

Or:

Alternating between standing on the spot while the teacher plays a melody on the recorder accompanied by children playing crotchets on percussion instruments, and, moving freely about the room without playing the instruments while the teacher accompanies, this time on a percussion instrument. Different accompaniment rhythms denote different ways of moving. The speed should adjust itself on each occasion to the age of those taking part. The running speed is not always twice as fast as that for walking. ♩ ♩ =

walking, ♫ ♫ =running, ♪.♪ ♪.♪ or ♩♪♩♪ = skipping or galloping.

If there should be an acoustic difference between skipping and galloping then two different instruments can be used, e.g. sleigh bells and coconut shells.

When reacting to different accompanying rhythms the children can move either in a circle, freely about the room or in snake formation.

Or:

They are divided into as many groups as there are rhythms and to each rhythm only one group moves at a time, the others 'bouncing' on the spot.

Or:

The children sit on the floor in a circle, one child is called out and moves round the edge of the circle in the appropriate way. When it is the next child's turn the rhythm is changed. The other children give the pulse in either clapping or patschen.

Instead of playing the accompanying rhythm the teacher can call out the appropriate terms such as 'walk', 'trot' or 'gallop'.

Changing both form and type of movement:

The teacher accompanies alternately on two different instruments, e.g. tambourine and bongos, one signifying moving in a circle, the other moving in snake formation or freely about the room. In addition there is a free change of rhythmic pattern on each instrument to which the children must react with appropriate steps.

Reaction to optical stimuli means in this case taking up and imitating another's (at first the teacher's) movement. It can be practised on the spot or while travelling.

The former is most easily achieved when the teacher stands facing all the children and makes simple movements that the children imitate mirror-wise. For instance: lifting one arm straight above the head, the other stretched out to the side, changing the position, at first one arm at a time, and then both arms simultaneously, big, slow arm movements and so on, so far everything without any metrically bound structure. This can be followed by simple ostinati with sound gestures, marking time with the feet on the spot in simple rhythmic patterns, walking forwards and backwards, to the right and to the left, all of which can be combined in longer metric structures. It is advisable, particularly with beginners, to repeat some phrases often and only gradually to make any changes.

When practising this while travelling it is best for the teacher to stand with the children in a circle. In this formation all the ways of moving that the children already know can be loosely connected together. It is important that each sequence be maintained at least until all the children can do it properly, that the changes of movement follow one another logically, and that the whole is executed in a lively way and with dynamic variety.

Different ways of moving: walking in a circle forwards, backwards or sideways, on tip-toe or using the whole foot, without or with a change of direction, the inclusion of sound gestures, transitions to running or skipping, changing to another formation or to a different time structure, or whatever other ideas occur on the spur of the moment to the person in charge.

Quick reaction also demands the adjustment to a rhythmic or movement sequence: One child, standing apart from the others, starts with a clapped rhythm or with a combination of sound gestures, or with a simple locomotive movement of its own selection. The other children are called out one after the other to join this child in either a stationary line or in moving snake formation and to pick up and imitate the rhythm or locomotive movement as quickly as possible. What matters is the speed with which each child finds the right connection. In the first movement lessons the same reaction exercises should often be given to encourage a quick reaction. Slight differences in the disposition of the task demand renewed attention.

110

Gymnastic exercises

At first sight gymnastic exercises seem to have no direct connection with Schulwerk activities. There are some, however, that should be made use of when we are concerned with awakening a feeling for relaxed posture and a flow of movement in rhythmic exercises, instrumental or conducting exercises, or, after considerable exertion to relax respectively certain joints or the whole body, or to prepare for springy running and leaping.

Preparation for rhythmic, instrumental and conducting exercises:

A prerequisite for relaxed music making is a relaxed posture. This has to be worked for constantly, particularly at first, until it becomes a habit.

The feeling for correct posture is most easily impressed upon the mind through developing it out of its opposite, slovenly posture:

When seated, all crumpled up like 'weary children', and by gradually straightening the spine until an alert posture is reached, as 'wide-awake children'. Both kinds of posture are alternated several times.

Quite as important is the movability of the arms in all their joints, so that flowing movement is possible:

Shoulders slowly pushed forward and pulled backwards, pushed high and pulled low, circling the shoulders in both directions with arms hanging or spread out sideways.

Arms raised forward to shoulder height, elbows gently curved and finger tips of both hands lightly touching; slowly bring the elbows to touch one another and apart again. Let this lead to making a quarter circle with each elbow.

Moving the hands up and down, to right and left and circling in both directions.

Bending and stretching movements of the wrist combined with the up and down, forwards and backwards and sideways movement of the whole arm. Impulsive spreading of all fingers in alternation with making a tight fist.

Free arm movements, parallel to one another, in contrary motion and independently from one another.

A frequently arising mistake is the pressing of elbows into the sides whether in clapping, instrumental or conducting exercises. The following exercises may be helpful:

Sitting cross-legged with hands on knees, lift the elbows and let them fall again, emphasising the lift. Starting with a slow tempo accelerate gradually ('beating with your wings'). Use the same movement allowing the hands to bounce away from the knees. Use the same movement without touching the knees at all, the hands not too near the body.

Standing with feet slightly apart, or sitting on stools or chairs, continuing with the movability of the elbows let the arms (from a horizontal position, held pointing forwards at shoulder height and slightly rounded) sink slowly until the hands touch the thighs, and raise them again feeling the movement start in the upper arm, continue with the lower arm and finish with the hand.

The same movement as the last one but in a faster tempo and as a falling movement, so that as soon as the hands touch the thighs they rebound to the starting position.

The same sequence of movement, each one interspersed with a rebounding pushing gesture at shoulder height. (This movement is a good preparation for beating in two-four time.)

Relaxation exercises:

Let the arms hang at the sides absolutely relaxed and shake them, in front, to the side and above the head.

Shake the hands with very loose wrists in all directions ('sprinkling water').

With feet apart let the trunk fall forward and with an up and down bouncing movement or with small turning movements relax the spine. Return slowly to the upright position.

Shake each leg forwards, to the side and backwards ('throw them away').

With feet together, bending the knees and ankles, bounce up and down until the floor is reached, and then up again without a sound (the arms hang loosely by the sides).

Bouncing exercises to prepare for springy running and leaping:

With feet together 'give' slightly at the knees.

With straight knees lift the heels off the floor until standing on the toes, then return heels to the floor with a slight bending of the knees; with an increase of tempo this becomes a jump.

Bounce alternately on right and left foot.

As a frequent intervening exercise:

Stretch, and twist in all directions.

Where there is room enough, let the children have a quick run all over the room, or circle once round their instrument either running, skipping or galloping.

Movement training

The different ways of moving, that have been treated in the reaction exercises in a more or less untechnical way, now require, as the teaching proceeds, a more technical training with rhythmic, dynamic and spatial variety in order to arrive at a security in the performance of given and original formal tasks.

Walking

In a movement lesson walking is usually not so popular with children as are running or skipping, and yet it can be varied in so many different ways that it can always be interesting. One can walk fast or slowly, with short or long steps, on the toes, the heels or on the outsides of the feet, with bent knees, in a squatting position in Russian dancer style, with straight knees or with raised, bent knees, heavily accented or lightly creeping, and in many other ways.

One can also walk in different time structures, the simplest being two-four and three-four time, followed later by other possibilities. The different character and the relationship of the stresses of the individual time structures are experienced in the movement.

Paths can be traced, curved or straight, forms can be made from changes of direction, and from changes of the mover's frontal relationship to the direction. These are at first tried out in walking and later used with running, skipping or galloping. There are additional possibilities for combining with clapping, small percussion, sound gestures, singing or recorder. The presentation of all these possibilities justifies the disproportionately large share taken here by walking.

Walking in curved paths

The circle, snake formation and free movement about the room have already been mentioned in connection with the reaction exercises.

Further exercises could be divided as follows:

Travelling individually in a small circle round one's own spot with choice of direction.

The same, in a predetermined direction.

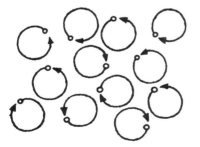
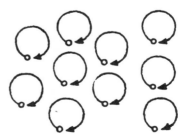

Walking in a large figure-of-eight, made easy at first by marking the centre point of each half of the eight.

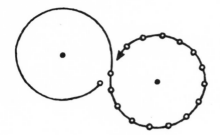

Walking individually in small figures-of-eight with free choice of direction.

The same in a predetermined direction.

New possibilities for walking in curved shapes can be arrived at through the placing of obstacles, that, after a certain amount of practice, can be left out.

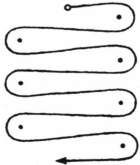

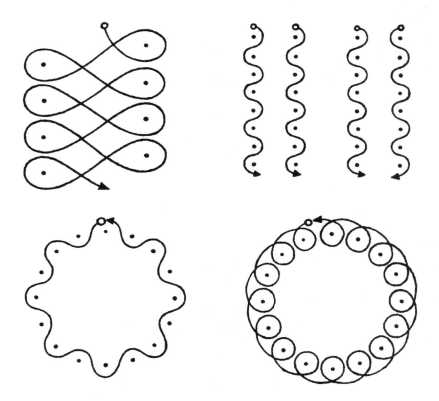

Walking in straight lines

Walking in straight lines can be executed forwards, backwards, sideways, singly, in pairs or in rows holding hands in different ways, in parallel or contrary direction, or crossing over.

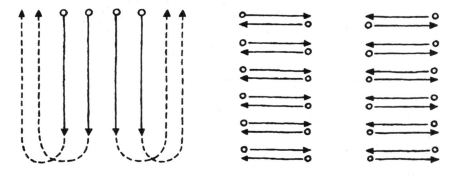

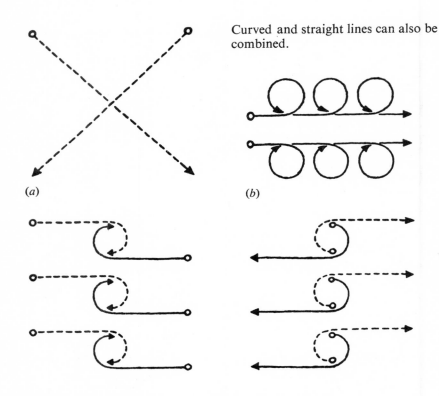

Curved and straight lines can also be combined.

(a)   (b)

Walking forward and backwards with a change of direction

Before using predetermined sequences such as are given in the exercises that follow, practice in change of direction should be given in the form of reaction exercises, in which precision is not yet of particular importance. The children are free to choose the manner in which they move and they usually arrive at skilful solutions themselves.

When using predetermined lengths of phrase it is easier if the changes come always after the same number of beats. (Keep the phrases short!) In the following examples the movement direction is indicated by an arrow,

f. = *forwards* *b* = *backwards*

the step-rhythm in notation.

♩ = *right foot*   ♩ = *left foot*

116

Speaking a suitable verse of the same length as the phrase in question,

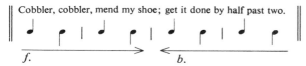

can make it easier to achieve the change at the right moment; equally an accent produced by a clap on the first or last step respectively, or a supporting accompaniment provided by the teacher.

When the two phrases are unequal the most straightforward proportions should at first be chosen.

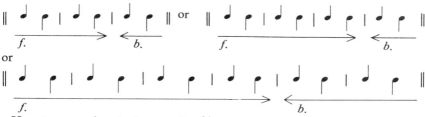

Here too a spoken text, or parts of it,

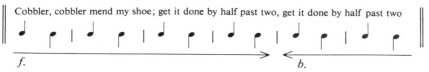

will be helpful towards feeling the exact moment of change; a rhyme thought of on the spur of the moment, or an improvised melody can serve the same purpose. Dynamic differences between going forwards and backwards arise practically from themselves. On no account should it come to the counting of steps, and thereby to a mechanical, wooden performance. A feeling for the form as a whole, even when it is such a small one, should be aroused and should be continually trained through each fresh task.

With further development any number of new structures can follow, perhaps also with changes of time, that, through the support of a suitable accompaniment, can be learnt with increasing ease and accepted as a matter of course.

Walking forwards and backwards with a change of front

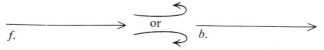

The movement direction remains the same, but at any given time a half-turn is made to change from walking forwards to walking backwards. This can be made to the right (left shoulder leads)

a half turn to the right on the first step

or to the left (right shoulder leads)

a half turn to the left on the first step

The start and finish of the half-turn is made clear by the position of the curved arrow and its relationship to the notation.

The children should be allowed to try out the different possibilities without thinking too consciously. Each will soon find out for himself the most comfortable way of doing it. The aim is to get a flowing sequence of movement, so one does not at first insist upon the direction in which the turns should be made. The teacher decides when the children are ready to take pleasure in working out a precise and predetermined movement sequence.

In the following examples mostly rhythmic variants are shown. The direction of the turn is given in each instance but is only to be taken as an indication of the simplest kind. It is also possible from time to time to turn in the opposite direction.

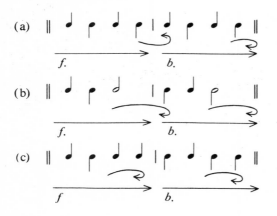

118

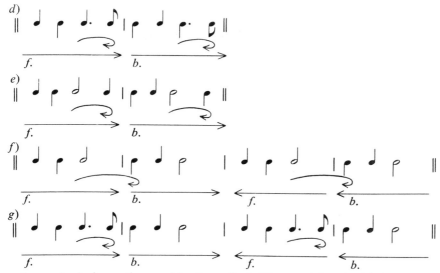

Example c) shows the combination of a half-turn with a double bounce, a twofold, even rebound on the same foot; example d) with a skip; example e) is similar but in a different time structure; the last two examples combine change of front and change of direction.

One must not allow oneself to be put off by all these diagrams. The examples are really very easy once the initial difficulties of translating them into movement sequences has been overcome. After some practice it will be possible to understand the movement sequence clearly, direct from the diagram.

Walking sideways

The simplest form is a slipping step executed in walking.

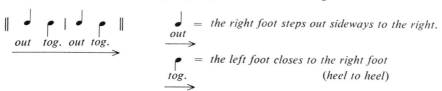

The arrows under the notes, without the additional f. and b., indicate the direction of the sideways movement.

A second possibility is for the following foot to cross over. The cross-over step can occur in front of or behind the leading foot, or with both these possibilities in alternation. When practising this the hips and knees twist and turn slightly in the direction of the movement but the pelvis should remain facing front.

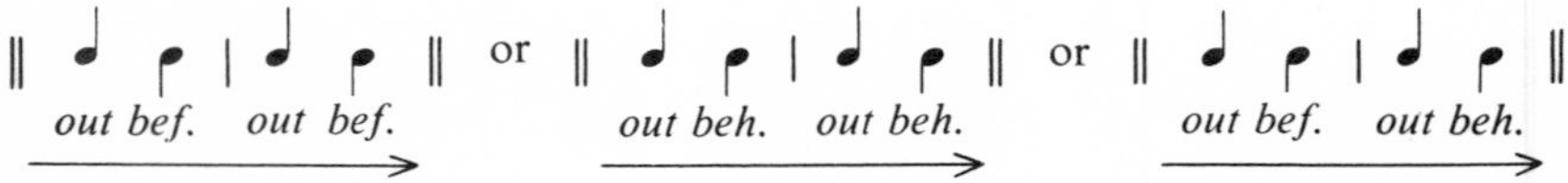

out bef.   out bef.   out beh.   out beh.   out bef.   out beh.

out

see above

$\int$
bef.
= a crossover step, left foot moving to right in front of right foot

$\int$
beh.
= a crossover step, left foot moving to right behind right foot

The cross-over step can start the sequence:

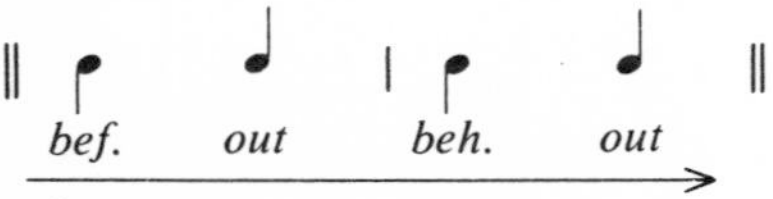

bef.   out   beh.   out

Structures in other rhythms and time units are also possible:

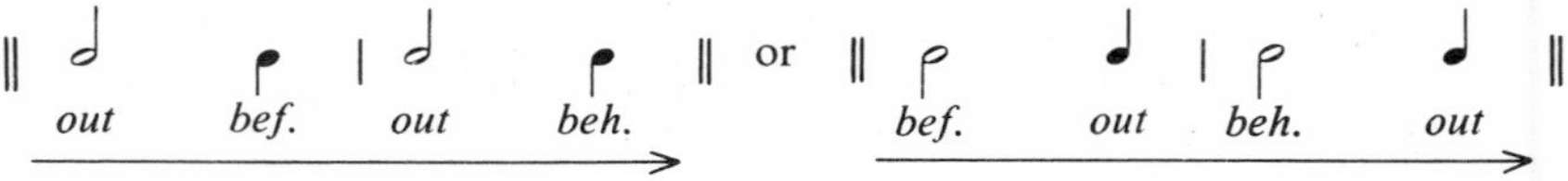

out   bef.   out   beh.   bef.   out   beh.   out

(skipping)

out   bef.   out   beh.

(galloping)

out bef. out beh. out bef. out beh.

120

Walking sideways in slipping step with change of direction

The simplest possibilities are:

The last closing up step before the change of direction carries no weight:

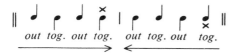

out tog. out tog.   out tog. out   tog.

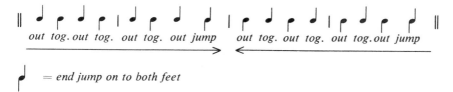

A small jump just before the change:

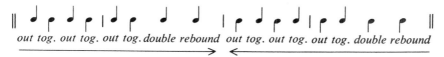

out tog. out tog.   out tog.   out jump   out tog. out tog.   out tog. out jump

= end jump on to both feet

A double rebound on the last step:

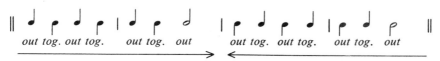

out tog. out tog. out tog. double rebound out tog. out tog. out tog. double rebound

A point of rest on the last step:

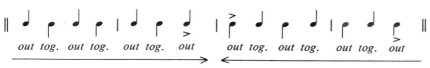

out tog. out tog.   out tog.   out   out tog.   out tog.   out tog.   out

Shortening the sequence by leaving out the last beat:

out tog. out tog.   out tog.   out   out tog. out tog.   out tog.   out

Where appropriate cross-over steps should be used with these examples. Some further possibilities:

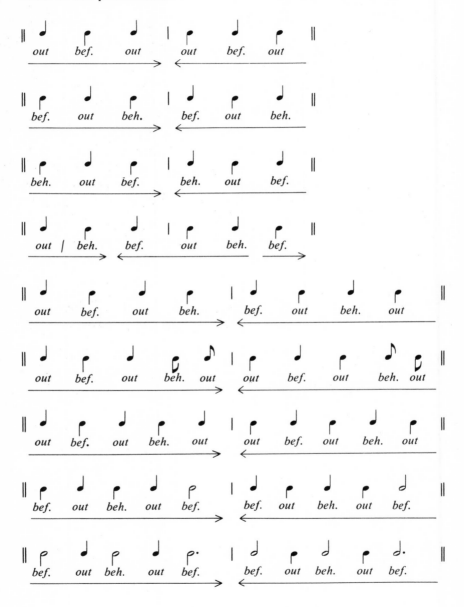

bef.   out   beh.   out   bef. out   beh.   bef.   out   beh.   out   bef. out   beh.

Walking sideways in slipping steps with change of front

The direction of movement remains the same, the change of front being achieved through a half-turn forwards (the front turns in the direction concerned) or backwards (the back turns in the direction concerned).

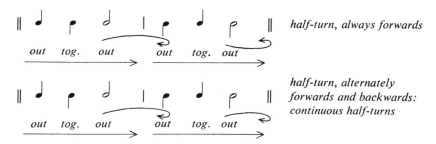

half-turn, always forwards

half-turn, alternately forwards and backwards: continuous half-turns

Variations:
Different phrase lengths:

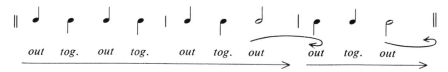

Combination of a half-turn with a rebound, the half-turn being made forwards each time:

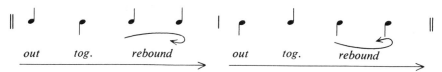

The same, but with the half-turn being made alternately forwards and backwards:

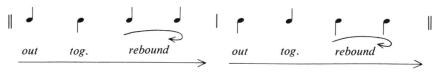

Combination of half-turn and skip, the half-turn being made forwards each time:

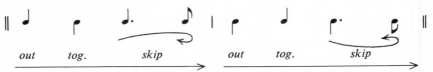

The same, but the half-turn alternately forwards and backwards:

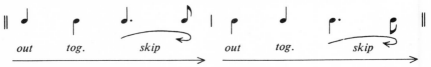

Variations for the cross-over step:
The half-turn comes alternately forwards and backwards:

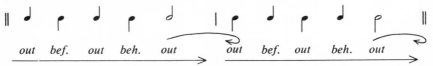

The half-turn always made forwards:

The combination of half-turn and skip:

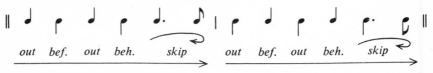

The skip in a different rhythm:

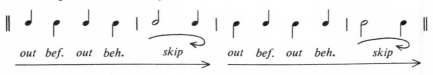

These examples should be increased through individual variations and combinations.

124

Walking with clapping and small percussion

Accompanying one's own walking, at first with clapping (snapping) in different rhythms, later with small percussion, aims at the independence of the walking step and the accompaniment when combined in a continuous movement. In the beginning the children mark time on the spot—particular emphasis must be given to each step so that the child is really aware of his own walking rhythm—and this is accompanied by clapping, at first in the same rhythm as the feet and then in minims (or giving the effect of minims). Other accompaniment patterns such as one- and two-bar ostinati are then added (see the chapter 'Rhythmic Building Bricks', p. 24 ff.).

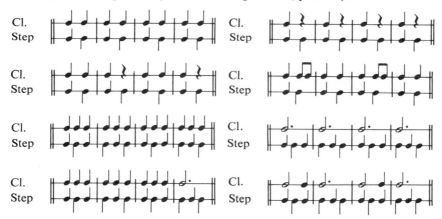

Marking time on the spot changes to travelling round the room, and the former emphasis is resolved into a flowing movement to which the teacher can play a melody on the recorder. Rhythmic echo-play and question and answer, as well as the clapping of freer rhythms, can now be tried in combination with walking. The steady metric pulse supplied by the feet provide a new basis for being made aware of the rhythms.

From the simplest ostinato accompaniments on one instrument, bigger forms that have already been created can now develop, and with more instruments.

An example: One can begin by using hand drums (tambours) struck alternately with the base of the thumb and the fingers (see p. 181), at first standing still, then combined with marking time on the spot and finally while walking round in a circle:

Then all the children strike only with the base of the thumb or only with the fingers:

When dividing into two groups each group first plays their rhythms alone, and then both groups play together. Every alternate child in the circle belongs to the same group so that a pair of children standing next to one another make the complete ostinato. Over this the teacher improvises a recorder melody. The part played by the fingers is now taken over by the claves, and the ostinato pattern is changed slightly, while the teacher's melody has a predetermined length of eight bars. The rests in the fourth and eighth bars in the tambour and clave parts are filled in with two cymbal clashes and, to give a sound foundation to the whole, a bass drum (stationary, in a central position) is added:

This is used as the A part of a rondo. The teacher provides a B part in the form of a recorder melody

to which a child improvises on a tambourine while the rest of the group stand in their places. A C part could perhaps consist only of rhythm and take the form of a 'conversation' between two children, one on tambour and the other on claves

Simple spatial structures in the form of a procession can easily be found by teacher and children together. Individual forms, also using other time units, should be tried out for oneself.

126

Walking with combined sound gestures and singing

While walking, combined sound gestures can be executed in many different ways and thus bring rhythmic vitality to the walking. A suitable starting point is provided by alternate stamping and clapping. It is first tried out on the spot with the stamp accent given always with the same foot, then with alternate feet, this changing to using the stamp as a means of travelling freely forwards, backwards or sideways. Tempo and dynamic level are varied. The following examples show various spatial and rhythmic possibilities:

127

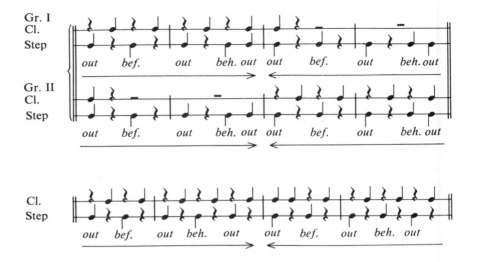

Other ostinato accompaniments with clapping, patschen and snapping respectively present new possibilities:

The steps can go forwards or sideways, can be closing up or crossing over steps, can remain in the same direction or can change direction, can go in straight or curved lines.

128

The ostinati that have so far consisted of one or two bars in length are now extended. Simple melodies for singing to these extended accompaniments now make complete a natural unity of movement, accompanying sound gestures and melody.

Various dispositions for these exercises are possible:
In close formation, the teacher opposite;
freely distributed round the room singly, or in pairs;
in a circle.

The combination of walking and sound gestures should also be practised in three-four time:

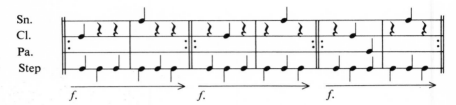

Doubling the pace of the walking tempo offers new possibilities. Here are some further examples in duple time:

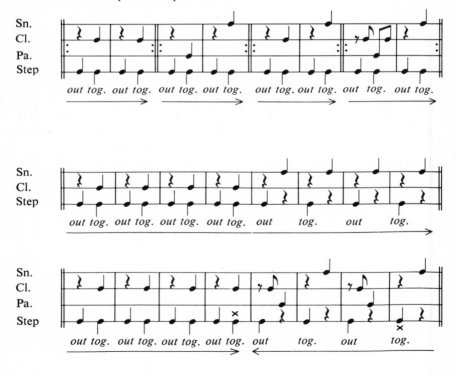

Walking with the recorder

As soon as the foundation for controlling a steady stream of breath and maintaining a good tone has been laid, then the recorder should also be played from time to time while walking.
The first exercises could be:

Walking freely round the room while playing a long, steadily held note for as long as the breath lasts.

Dividing a sustained note into successive minims.

Short ostinato accompaniments using two and more notes,

to which the teacher, leading them in a simple way around the room, plays a melody.

From ostinato accompaniments of one or more bars two- and three-note melodies are developed.

Instead of only travelling forwards, walking sideways and backwards, changing direction, turning on the spot and walking in curved lines are included.

Phrases of walking *and* playing the recorder and walking without playing the recorder, each phrase being of equal length, can alternate with one another.

As progress is made the range of melody notes is more and more extended, and the rhythms become more varied.

All suitable melodies, particularly processional music, small dance songs and similar pieces can be played while walking, provided that they have been mastered both technically and musically.

An aim for more advanced students is to improvise melodies while walking, at first completing phrases started by the teacher, and then making up their own complete improvisations.

Running

Running can be practised in many different ways: in forwards, sideways and backwards directions; in curved or straight lines; in near-the-ground, far-reaching steps; in high-stepping and very light, or near-the-ground and very heavy steps; individually, in pairs, in rows or groups, in different lengths of phrase and kinds of time structure. All examples in the section headed 'Walking' (p. 113 ff.) that refer to spatial patterns, changes of front and direction, can be transferred to running, though the combinations with sound gestures and small percussion are only possible to a limited extent. The transition from walking to running and vice versa should be particularly carefully practised. The most suitable tempo for this transition from the one kind of movement to the other has to be discovered for oneself.

Hopping and Skipping

Hopping on one foot is a matter of practice in skill and balance. It is possible for quite small children and is used with pleasure in the early stages of teaching.

Various ways of using it in play:

—with one or both hands hold one ankle behind the body, the relevant knee being bent double;
—hold one knee while it is held forward and high and bent double;
—stretch the free leg out forwards, backwards or to the side;
—for the well-practised: turn in circles on the spot with the free leg held out sideways, and change the direction by landing on the floor with both feet (feet apart) and starting immediately to turn in the opposite direction using the other foot.

The children should be allowed to discover other possibilities for themselves. In order not to strain the ankles, hopping should not be practised for too long at a stretch and should soon give place to skipping on alternate feet:

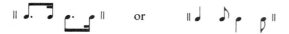

All the following examples refer to skipping. They can be practised:
—in short steps with the knees held high;
—in long 'flying' steps;
—forwards, backwards, sideways, turning on the spot;
—individually, in pairs or in rows;
—in different spatial forms such as circle, snake, etc.;

All the examples in the section headed 'Walking' (p. 113 ff.) concerning change of direction and front can be used for skipping. Rhythmic variations are possible:

Instead of skipping continually, within any one sequence only some steps are skipped:

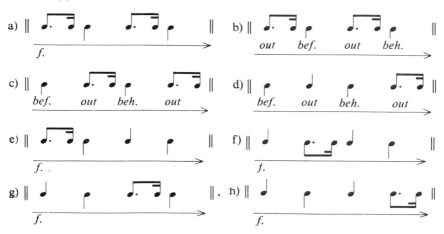

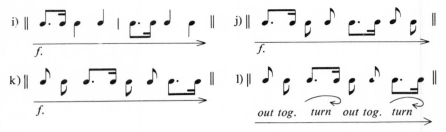

or:

—a sequence is begun with an up beat:

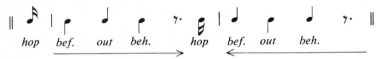

Further variations for skipping forwards, backwards and sideways as well as those for turning on the spot should be discovered for oneself. During all practice give attention to lightness and to a relaxed posture.

Bouncing

Ways of practising:

—Bounce on both feet through slight bending and straightening of the knee joints, the entire sole of the foot remains touching the floor. Increase the range of movement until the feet come away from the floor.

—Bounce in alternation between the feet so that the toes of one foot are always lightly touching the floor; the action of the foot is a rolling one— from tiptoe to ball, to heel.

—From bouncing on the spot change to small bouncing running steps in all directions.

Double bounce or rebound: two even bounces on each foot:

Double bounces can occur forwards, backwards and sideways, with changes of direction and front and with steps of different sizes and speeds.

Some examples in a sideways direction:

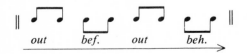

134

Double bounces can be practised in continuous half-turns both forwards and backwards

or sideways.

In order to maintain a straight line one must keep the eyes focused in the direction of travel for as long as possible, and, after a half-turn, return them again in this direction as soon as possible.

One can find out for oneself the various possibilities of changing direction frequently, or at more widely spaced intervals, at regular or at irregular intervals, at steadily maintained or at varying dynamic levels. Double bounces—three or more of these are also possible on each foot—are particularly suitable in combination with walking and running. Here also the children should be given many opportunities to experiment with and find new forms of their own while the teacher plays a melody.

Various ways of holding the free leg in double bounces:

—stretching it out forwards, backwards and sideways;
—forwards, with bent knee;
—for the more advanced: the free leg is stretched and moves from a backwards to a forwards position (when travelling forwards) and from a forwards to a backwards position (when travelling backwards); alternation of bending and stretching (and stretching and bending) the knee when travelling forwards, and so on.

Jumping

This can be practised in various ways:

—from both feet on to both feet,
—from one foot on to the other foot,
—from one foot on to both feet,
—from both feet on to one foot.

A powerful jump from one foot on to the same foot is also possible.

Jumps from both feet on to both feet (that can be done with or without an intervening bounce) are tried out by every physically active child at an early age and these take on various forms:

—feet together on the spot;
—feet together travelling forwards;
—feet together in combination with quarter, half and whole turns on the spot;
—feet together when jumping forwards and backwards, to the right and to the left, and also forwards, to the right, backwards to the left (without intervening bounce);
—feet together, jumping forwards in a squatting position;
—feet together, jumping with the knees held high;
—feet together, kicking both heels behind;
—landing feet together but while jumping kicking one heel behind and stretching the other leg out in front;

136

—alternating between feet apart and feet together, at the same time lifting
and dropping the arms (jumping Jack or puppet);

—landing with feet in the walking position and alternate feet leading;

—landing with feet apart but bringing them together quickly while in the air.

Jumps from one foot to the other can come in the following forms:

—with the free leg stretched forwards (forwards scissors);

—with the free leg stretched backwards (backwards scissors);

—with the knees held high;

—running, forward jumps (achieved through the strong way each foot lands
and takes off again), the emphasis laid either on high or long jumps, and
done consecutively without any intervening steps.

—the same, but with intervening steps and in various rhythmic patterns:

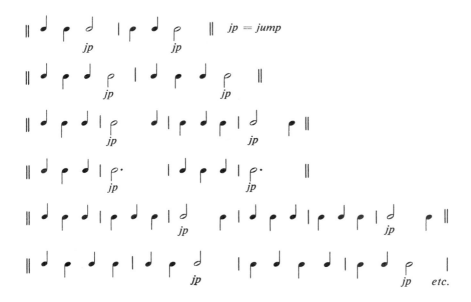

—running jumps in combination with half-turns and changes of direction:

—running jumps that turn successively:

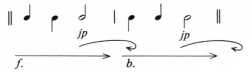

Preparation for turning jumps:
—sideways steps with change of direction;

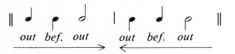

—in combination with two half-turns, at first without, then with a jump on the first step.

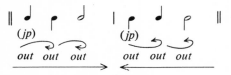

—in a changed rhythm,

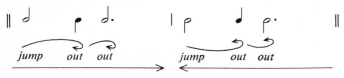

—with a skip before the change of direction.

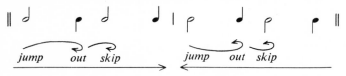

Continuous turning jumps: each sequence is introduced by one step out to the side followed by a closing up step:

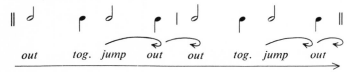

138

In jumps from one foot on to both feet the landing can be made with feet together or with feet apart.

Those with feet together are possible forwards or sideways, with and without intervening steps. The free leg is held straight:

—forwards, without intervening steps:

ρ = *landing on both feet*

—forwards, with intervening steps:

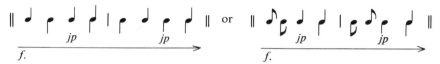

—continuously sideways:

—sideways with a change of direction:

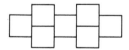

Jumps that land with feet apart can be done as in one version of 'hop-scotch'. As a preliminary aid paving stones can be drawn on the floor.

Jumps from both feet on to one foot can be made starting either with feet together or with feet apart.

Starting with feet together the jump can be practised with various positions for the free leg:
—pointing backwards with bent knee,
—pointing forwards with bent knee held high,
—pointing forwards and held straight.

Landing always on the same foot is just as possible as landing alternately first on one foot and then on the other.

In jumps starting with feet apart the free leg is held pointing backwards with bent knee. All jumps can be made on the spot or while travelling.

Galloping

Galloping, that really belongs under the heading of jumping, takes a specially favoured place in movement lessons with children and is therefore treated separately. Together with skipping with which it shares a dotted rhythm—though with galloping the jump is made from one foot to the other—

it is a way of moving that is used very frequently in the early stages of movement teaching.

Galloping is practised forwards and sideways. (Children who cannot yet gallop are asked, before they start to move, to put one leg forward. This leg should then remain in front throughout this particular galloping sequence.)

Galloping forwards can make use of long steps that are near the ground or of short steps with the knees held high, or of a small and big gallop in alternation

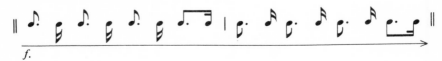

and called 'little-big gallop'.

A good posture can be achieved through imagining the position of the rider. The hands hold imaginary reins or riding whip. 'Riding around' imaginary or real objects helps to train awareness of space and direction (see sketches for curved pathways on p. 113).

In 'dressage' one can change from left-footed gallop (left foot begins) to right-footed gallop by means of a skip:

140

The sideways gallop

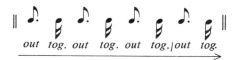

out tog. out tog. out tog./out tog.

should be practised with the feet turned slightly outwards to avoid the danger of turning the ankles over.

It can be practised individually, or in pairs holding hands, either beside one another or opposite, in straight or in curved lines.

A change of direction in the sideways gallop can occur by means of a skip,

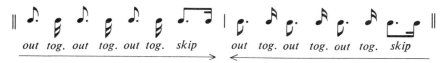

out tog. out tog. out tog. skip   out tog. out tog. out tog. skip

through a closing-up step with no transfer of weight before the change,

out tog. out tog. out tog.   out tog. out tog. out tog.

or through a jump on to both feet,

out tog. out tog. out jp land   out tog. out tog. out jp land

Maintaining the same direction but with a change of front:

out tog. out tog. out tog. skip   out tog. out tog. out tog. skip

out tog. out tog. out tog. skip   out tog. out tog. out tog. skip

This is also possible with a partner: back to back, the leading hand holds that of its partner. At the half-turn they swing down between the two partners to take up the opposite position.

Sideways gallop in combination with skipping:

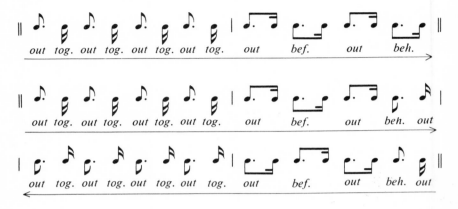

It is not difficult to find other possible combinations of galloping and skipping for oneself.

Swaying

The different ways of swinging the body (pendulum, circle, figure of eight and tilting) and of swinging the arms and legs as practised in a gymnastic training, go beyond the scope of an elementary movement education. They are therefore not considered here. On the other hand, a gentle rocking movement that helps one to feel the buoyancy of the three- and six-beat barring is particularly suitable, and is reserved for particular use with girls:

Changing the weight between right and left foot with a swaying movement —with feet together, or with one a little in front of the other—the sideways step and close and the cross-over step, also these in combination with a half-turn are basic possibilities.

The simultaneous speaking of a series of words,

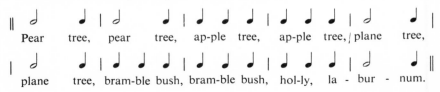

142

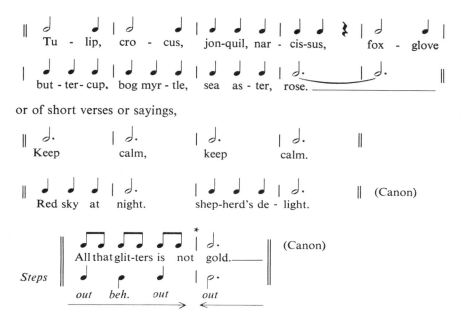

Tu - lip, cro - cus, jon-quil, nar - cis-sus, fox - glove but - ter- cup, bog myr - tle, sea as - ter, rose.

or of short verses or sayings,

Keep calm, keep calm.

Red sky at night. shep-herd's de - light. (Canon)

Steps

All that glit-ters is not gold. (Canon)

out beh. out out

or the humming or singing of two alternating notes or simple melodies,

Humming or Singing

Humming or Singing

ad. lib vocal acc.

can support the swing of the movement and at the same time lead uncon-sciously to correct breathing.

Movement variations and combinations

So far, in the presentation of each different way of moving, through change of direction or change of front, simple, spatial and at the same time dynamic variations of a movement form and the combination of various ways of moving have arisen. In this section, for the more experienced, a few examples that show further possibilities of development and variation are given. The examples are melodies (some in major and minor keys) with drum accompaniment that can be extended, varied, or used only as a stimulus to individual experiment. Before proceeding to a fixed movement form each particular way of moving should be practised separately and then freely combined in reaction exercises.

Running and bouncing

The first example: a two-bar movement pattern

is the basis of the first sequence. It can be done in a circle or along the diagonals of the room. Attention should be paid to a clear start that should arise from an alert and buoyant posture and both performance and adjustment to one another should seem easy and natural. All variations should also flow naturally and feel physically right. The example of the teacher can provide a stimulus. The possibility of changing the movement patterns by reacting to directions given by the teacher should also not be neglected. These directions should be short and precise.

Variations such as the following can be developed from the foregoing basic example:
—running forwards—bouncing backwards,
—running backwards—bouncing forwards,
—running forwards—bouncing on the spot,

—running forwards—bounce while turning on the spot,
—running forwards—bounce on two successive half-turns,
—instead of four running steps, only two:

—three running steps instead of two:

Variations of the basic pattern in a sideways direction:

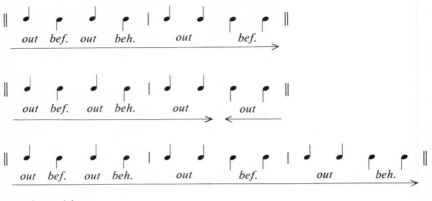

together with:

together with:

or:

Continuous three-four time with skipping, jumping and turning

In this section skipping is notated in the following rhythm:

Changing from walking in three time to skipping within an eight bar phrase:

together with:

Shortened to half the length and the variation: six steps forwards, each skip combined with a half-turn:

together with:

Instead of the two skips a half-turn with a jump, followed by a skip on the spot, the whole sequence repeated in the opposite direction:

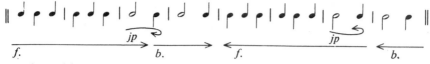

together with:

The same basic form, but at the repetition in the opposite direction the six steps are omitted:

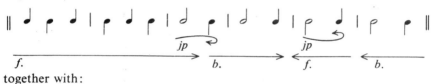

together with:

Each group of three steps now contains a half-turn, the skips always travelling forwards:

Variations in a sideways direction can easily be found for oneself.

149

Step variations in five-four time

A rhythm in five-four time, that is more likely to arise through the chance alteration of some other rhythm, is practised systematically with those who are more experienced.

The natural stresses of two- and three-four can be retained

or the whole bar can be considered as a unity without any dividing stresses.

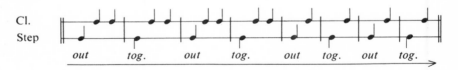

In the following example a division of three-four and two-four bars is given as a basis.

At first, through stamping and clapping on the spot, the change from three- to two-four time is made freely, then in four-bar sequences

and next combined with step and close in a sideways direction.

together with:

---

* This is not an ideal solution, but I have yet to find an English word of five syllables with a genuine stress on the first syllable. (M. M.)

150

From now on the two kinds of time alternate,

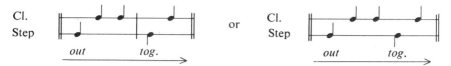

together with:

Another step-rhythm is first practised by itself,

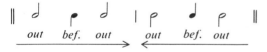

together with:

then in combination with the previous step-rhythm.

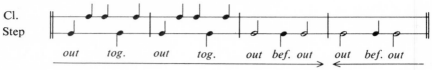

together with:

The new step-rhythm is now done in a forwards and backwards direction

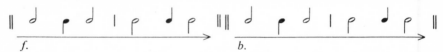

and each half is then given a different dynamic level. Later, in the forward moving phrase the first of each bar is marked with a jump.

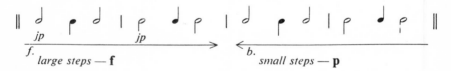

The jump then contains a half-turn and the following steps are done backwards, thus maintaining the direction. The sequence is then repeated in the opposite direction.

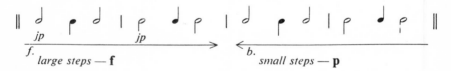

The movement sequence of the fourth from last example is combined with that of the last example. This is done by means of a quarter turn: to the right when going from the first to the second; to the left when going back from the second to the first. Each sequence is repeated. The following melody can be played:

Movement sequences combining two-two and three-four time

In a flowing tempo a pattern of steps is made using minims in two-two in alternation with crotchets in three-four time. From a free change from the one to the other, according to directions called out by the teacher, the following form is reached:

153

together with:

This is first done freely about the room, then in particular spatial and rhythmic sequences:

—all steps forwards,

—all steps backwards,

—the two-two bars forwards, the three-four bars backwards,

—the two-two bars forwards, the three-four bars turning (three steps for a half-turn).

Sideways:

—the two-two bars as side and cross-over steps, the three-four bars turning (three steps for a half-turn),

—in a different step rhythm and with a change of direction by means of a skip, also with a jump at the beginning of the first three-four bar,

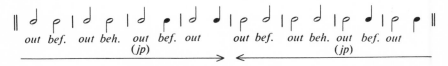

—in the same rhythmic sequence but with a turning jump in each three-four bar (maintaining the same direction of travel).

—The sequence is shortened.

together with:

Further movement sequences should be discovered for this melody.

Movement pieces

Movement pieces can have various starting points. These can be children's songs or spoken texts, instrumental pieces or dance songs. Starting points can also be provided by the way of moving itself, out of which a form can be made, to which later a specially composed rhythmic or melodic accompaniment can be added. In children's rhymes such as 'Cobbler, cobbler, mend my shoe', 'Jack be nimble', 'How many miles to Babylon?', and 'Wash, hands, wash', in which some kind of actions may arise naturally from the text, these actions should be developed from the children's imagination. The teacher should only help to create some form, so that an end result is achieved, and the children do not remain stuck at the improvisatory stage.

The same applies to short sayings that can be mimed in some way. Only texts that have some relationship to movement should be used.

In the first attempts at working out with children a movement form to music, be it instrumental piece or dance song, the children must have the opportunity to grasp and understand the overall structure and the individual parts so that they can react to these in movement. This reaction should first happen without their being tied to any kind of difficult spatial form—each child moves either freely about the room or with the others in a circle. One starts with clearly structured melodies with two phrases, decides upon a change of movement for the second phrase, and the time for making the change must be heard by every child.

For this only the simplest kinds of movement and spatial forms should be used: walking, running, skipping or galloping, individually or in pairs, forwards or backwards, freely about the room, in a big circle or in smaller circles, turning on the spot, sound gestures made while standing, and similar material.

An example for beginners:

156

SG.

SG.

AG.

AX.

Tri.

Timp.

Bass

From Orff-Schulwerk, *Music for Children*, Vol. I, Schott, London, p. 95.

The introduction is at first ignored. The teacher plays the melody on a recorder (the children later play accompaniments to it) while the children listen to the two phrases, each four bars long.

The movement could be as follows:

Part 1: Scattered round the room (or in circle formation) they clap an ostinato rhythm:

Cl.

Part 2: They skip freely about the room (or in circle formation) and arrive in a standing position at the end of the melody.

Or:

Part 1: Skipping freely about the room;

Part 2: with the nearest child as partner continuing to skip in a particular way, or skipping round and round with one another on the spot. When adding the four introductory bars these could be performed with sound gestures done on the spot:

Cl.
Pa.

Other possibilities should be tried out.

157

A further example for the more experienced:

From Orff-Schulwerk, *Music for Children*, Vol. I, Schott, London, p. 111. For accompaniments see same piece, No. 31, p. 111.

158

A group of children at the instruments accompanies a second group that dances.

The rondo has the following form:

A_1, first linking bars,
A_2, C, second link,
A_3, D, third link,
A_4.

To this the following movement is suggested:

A_1: in a big circle holding hands, continuous walking steps, three to a bar, speedy tempo. At the repetition of the melody move in the opposite direction.

B: Movement improvisation by one child, the rest kneel.

First linking bars: make two circles out of the one big one.

A_2: as A_1.
C: Either: in the centre of each circle one child turns and changes place with another at the repetition, or: one child improvises in the middle of each circle while the rest kneel.

Second link: make four circles out of the two circles.

A_3: as A_1.
D: All children move freely round the room.

Third link: All children form one big circle again.

A_4: as A_1.

An example of a canon in movement (for the more experienced):

Ding   dong dig-gi-dig-gi dong   dig-gi-dig-gi ding dang dong.

From Orff-Schulwerk, *Music for Children*, Vol. I, Schott, London, p. 24.

A four-bar movement sequence provides the basis:
Bar 1: a skip followed by three steps forward:

Bar 2: full-turn on the spot using four steps.
Bar 3: as Bar 1.
Bar 4: a half-turn using three steps, clapping at the same time in the step rhythm. The sequence is repeated.
Possible ways of performance:
In a two-part canon (the second entry after one bar): two concentric circles moving in opposite directions.
In a four-part canon (each entry coming after half a bar): two rows standing opposite to one another,

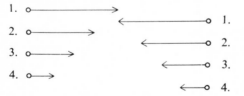

or individually, freely about the room.

In a movement piece that arises from the movement itself and has no music or text to give it a starting point, it is important to bring together one or more ways of moving in a clear form, whose parts bear some relation to one another.

The themes of movement pieces or studies of this kind can draw upon all types of movement. They can include running or skipping, swaying sequences and other possibilities. Music that is later composed for such pieces—it could be a purely rhythmic accompaniment—must follow the pattern of the movement.

An example: A movement piece with walking and skipping.
Formation: Two rows opposite one another, as many pairs as is necessary.

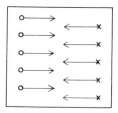

The movement piece that follows consists of five movement sequences each containing eight bars in four-four time. The two bars introduction are performed by everyone on the spot with sound gestures:

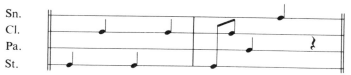

Sequence 1:
Bars 1 and 2: Holding hands the rows walk four steps towards one another and four steps back again.
Bars 3 and 4: Side and close to the right, and then to the left with a clap on beats 2 and 4.

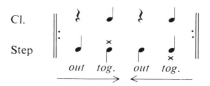

Bars 5 to 8: Repetition of bars 1 to 4.
Sequence 2:
Bars 1 to 4: Holding hands in rows walk four steps forwards towards one another; holding hands with opposite partners take eight steps to turn round with them; for the last four steps, holding hands in rows again, return backwards to original starting place.
Bars 5 to 8: Repetition of bars 1 to 4.

161

Sequence 3:

Bars 1 *to* 4: In eight steps change places with opposite partner, and, once there, use a further eight steps to turn round in a small circle.

Bars 5 *to* 8: Using the same sequence of steps return to starting place.

Sequence 4:

Three opposite pairs now change places, taking eight steps to do so. On arriving at the new position they turn once more to face their partner. Each pair starts one after the other at a bar's distance. In the last four bars they return to their original places in the same order. Those who do not move accompany with alternate patschen and clapping. The sequence will need to be adapted according to the number of pairs.

Sequence 5:

As sequence 1.

There are now eight transitional bars: In three times eight steps (6 bars) both rows take up a new formation. As they do this they snap their fingers on the first, third and fifth of every eight steps. In the seventh and eighth bars the groups remain in their new places and repeat the two introductory bars.

162

In the new position the whole dance of five sequences is repeated once more, this time skipping instead of walking. As an ending—the two introductory bars once more.

The melody that follows is suitable for both versions.

Sequence 1: Melody A

Sequence 2: Melody B

Sequence 3: Melody A

Sequence 4: Melody C

Sequence 5: Melody A

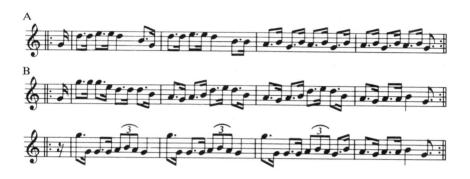

Elementary movement improvisation

There is some music that evokes a spontaneous movement response. It is mostly an unconscious motivation that is thus appealed to that is, particularly in a child, as yet untrained. This unconscious motivation should be fostered and encouraged. We must try to preserve that which is intuitive and original, but at the same time help to bring that which may at first be formless and haphazard to a conscious form. For this purpose music that gives an impulse to movement is a suitable medium. It should, particularly at first, be improvised by the teacher.

Movement improvisation should always start early. There will always be children who, in their carefree way, particularly enjoy moving freely, and who have an enlivening effect on other children. They also are mostly not afraid to move by themselves and to accompany their dance with singing. They forget the world around them and are completely absorbed in their dance. Especially when working with small groups teachers should dare to encourage more and more children to give free expression to their melodic

163

and movement imagination in this way. There are also children who lack the courage and self-confidence to move freely. One should not force such children but rather give them tasks where they feel more at home; to take over an accompanying part, or perhaps just to watch. The moment when the joy in movement overcomes the anxiety usually arises of itself. The teacher can be very helpful here with encouraging comments, indeed all criticism of improvisation should be positive.

It is advisable at first to allow all the children to improvise together or, where the numbers are too large, in groups. Here the children move as they like and as they feel to a melody played by the teacher. What results is at first fortuitous, without recognisable form, technically imperfect and mostly rather awkward. For a beginning, however, this is quite sufficient, the main thing is *that* it occurs and not *how* it occurs. The melody should have a clear, uncomplicated form that the children can understand, and on the rhythmic side it should give a stimulus to certain kinds of movement. (Melodies for walking, running, skipping, etc.)

In the first group improvisations each child moves for himself without reference to the others. It could then be suggested that they make contact with, and react to one another. Opportunities for moving together should be taken: running together in twos for a short stretch, making circles round one another or with one another, separating from one partner and making contact with a new one.

Boys should be given a chance to take part in movement improvisation in a way suitable to them that places more emphasis on a vigorous rhythm. The playing of claves or tambours while moving, or an improvisation on one or more timpani that can be built into a movement sequence provide activities that will interest boys.

The aim of the next stage is the development of a feeling for form, the feeling for proportion and length. The rondo in its most simple form with an equal length for all sections is the most suitable material for this.

For the following xylophone melody (the A part of a rondo) a movement sequence in which everyone can take part should be found. The intervening episodes (also to be discovered for oneself) can be solo improvisations:

164

Movement accompaniment

The aim and purpose of a movement accompaniment is both to support and stimulate the movement, whether through rhythm, melody, or both. The main criterion is that the accompaniment should be appropriate to the movement whether it takes the form of clapping or finger snapping, speech, humming or singing, or whether it is performed on an instrument.

The accompaniments that do not use instruments are the easiest to use since they do not demand particular technical skills. All instrumental accompaniments require a certain mastery of the instrument concerned. An intuitive understanding of the movement sequence, the ability to give it a shape and a feeling for dynamic range and tone quality are, however, always necessary. An accompaniment that remains always at the same level of intensity has a deadening effect, but one that is varied, and that keeps returning to very soft playing, stimulates attention. Complete cessation of the accompaniment here and there increases the attractiveness of the sound when it starts again; frequent changes of instrument guard against monotony of sound. An accompaniment that is too complicated diverts attention that should be given to observing and correcting the children; simple, clearly structured phrases lead to a clear form.

The rhythmic accompanying instruments most suitable for the teacher to use are: bongos, tambour, woodblock or tubular woodblock, and tambourine. In addition to these, particularly for swaying movement, a low-pitched tambour, hanging cymbal, various sizes of smaller cymbals and triangle.

The short bright sound of bongos is suitable for practically all types of movement except swaying. They are particularly attractive when a rhythm is cleverly divided between the two sounds of different pitch. The possibility of being able to change quickly to another instrument (to recorder, tambourine, or, when using beaters from rectangular to tubular woodblock) is a great advantage that has particular significance for reaction exercises. A resonant, not too small tambour is suitable for the accompaniment of all types of movement. It can be struck with a beater, or better, because of the much greater variety possible, with the hand.

The tubular woodblock with its two different pitches can be used in a similar way to the bongos. When accompanying movement it should as a rule be struck with hard felt beaters and not with wooden ones.

The rectangular woodblock with its hard sound should be used only sparingly when struck with wooden beaters.

The tambourine is often used, as appropriate to the character of its sound, for light movement in a quick rhythm.

Ways of moving such as walking, running and skipping, when these are practised in a continuous sequence, could be accompanied by the teacher in exact conformity with the pace and pattern of the steps, but it is nevertheless better to structure the accompaniment — the most simple way being in four- and eight-bar groupings — and thus unconsciously to train the children's feeling for form.

For walking (in a faster tempo also suitable for running):

166

For skipping or galloping:

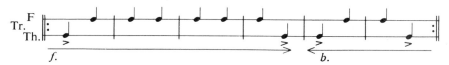

On the other hand, when a movement sequence has a particular form, then the accompaniment must make this form clear.

An example: A change from walking forwards to walking backwards in phrases of four and two bars respectively:

The children should soon be drawn into the activity of accompanying movement. They clap to the walking speed of the teacher who walks sometimes faster, sometimes slower, sometimes more heavily accentuated and then again very quietly, but who always makes each change very clearly as he proceeds around the room while the children try to adjust themselves immediately to every change of tempo and dynamics.

Or:

A group of children claps (or combines patschen with clapping, or stamping with clapping) in time to the walking speed of another group, while the teacher adds a melody on the recorder.

Through the fact that those who accompany and those who move are often exchanging places, the children soon learn to avoid the mistakes of which they themselves have become aware. The tempo must be correct, neither too fast nor too slow, and it may not fluctuate during an exercise that lasts for some time. It is important always to be watching the movement so that the accompaniment coincides with it.

Another possibility is the use in accompaniment of such instruments as claves, sleigh bells, rattles and shakers, triangles, small cymbals, hand drums and other small percussion.

The playing of crotchets alone will soon be extended through the use of one- or two-bar ostinati, and from there come to a free style in all known time structures led, at first, by the teacher's melody.

The most suitable instruments for the teacher to use as a melodic accompaniment to movement are the descant and treble recorder. The recorder has advantages over the barred instruments through the intensity of its tone and because it allows the teacher to observe the movement all the time, to move from one part of the room to another, to phrase the movement through the breath span of the melodic phrase, and to give variety through articulation. The use of the recorder as a solo instrument demands a good mastery of technique; when, however, other instruments are added as a foundation of sound colour, then it can be played in a simpler way.

As always, clear forms are necessary: easily remembered melodies that repeat exactly or nearly exactly, clear melodic cadences, frequent changes of pitch register (the lower register of the recorder should not be used too often) and always a lively delivery.

In his accompaniment for movement the teacher should also take into account the age of the children. For the very young he should give preference to pentatonic or major key melodies with simple rhythms and short phrases that repeat often; with older children he will use all major and minor modes and more discriminating rhythms.

The children's movement accompaniments on barred instruments begin with ostinato rhythms in octaves or fifths. Walking is accompanied at walking pace and the teacher's melody is added.

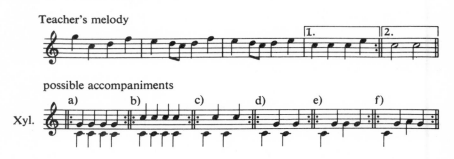

The same can be played at a faster tempo for running.

With skipping or galloping the teacher takes up the dotted rhythm in his melody while the children accompany in crotchets as in the previous example.

Teacher's melody

168

Later the children can also accompany in dotted rhythms that can be prepared through patschen.

The teacher's melody is freer over such an accompaniment.

Teacher's melody

The next stage is for the children to play melodies that they have learnt. First possibilities would be small pieces made from scale sections (see p. 70). Most of these are adaptable to every kind of movement so that the same melody, through rhythmic variation, can be played for walking, running, skipping or with a different time signature.

The individual pieces are short, and must therefore be lengthened for continuous movement practice. This can be achieved by playing the same melody in different registers or by its repetition by a different instrumental group, soft and loud, solo and tutti, without and with accompaniment. Two or more well-matching melodies can also be played one after the other so that the forms AB, ABA, ABC, ABACA etc. can arise.

The aim of melodic movement accompaniment by children is for them later to be able to improvise, whether on barred instruments or recorders.

The improvisation exercises in the first part of the book will serve as a start, and it needs only practice and a little courage to dare to take part in these exercises oneself. The main difficulty for the beginner lies in the fact that an improvisation of this kind usually lasts for a long time and his melodic invention and ability to make a shape cannot hold out to the end. One solution for this difficulty can be found in a rondo-like design with repetition of whole melodies or parts of melodies, or in an alternating contribution between two or more children so that each has only a phrase of four or eight bars to play. A continuous ostinato accompaniment on one or two instruments takes care of the continuity in any case, even if one player drops out. To avoid the danger of monotony the ostinato should be changed frequently. For improvisations of long duration two or more predetermined ostinati can exchange with one another, e.g.:

The change can take place in response to a sign, or after a predetermined time.

The improvisation of recorder melodies can be attempted in the same way.

The first attempts at improvisation for movement should be limited in duration, but, for this reason they should be repeated often.

Even if the well prepared guidance of a large group, the clear direction of the movement through the music remains the preserve of the teacher, nevertheless all attempts by the children to accompany their own movement and to develop their intuitive and creative abilities have their contribution to make. Here, as well, the children can experience the unity of movement and music.

Suggestions for movement lessons for beginners

(These are thought of as being suitable for children of from 4 to 6 years old.)

The first lesson:

The children distribute themselves about the room, each child moving freely, though without colliding with any of the others. The teacher accompanies at walking pace on a tambour. When the tambour stops the children stand still.

The same, walking backwards.

Once more, running forwards.

The children surround the teacher, holding hands in a small, tight circle. By everyone taking one or more steps backwards simultaneously the circle is made larger. They let go their hands. The movement that has already been practised is now tried in a circle.

The children now relax the upper half of their bodies by bending down to the floor and letting it hang limply. The teacher shows them how to do it.

The children sit on the floor or on stools in a circle or semi-circle. Every child from one to the next speaks his first name.

The same again clearly accentuated.

In the same way each child tries to clap his name. Suitable names are clapped by everyone: quietly, loudly, by small groups, by one child alone, by all.

The teacher shows the difference between clapping badly and clapping well. All the children clap even, continuous crotchets together with the teacher in varying degrees of volume, with gradual changes and with sudden ones.

The teacher names one of the children and all clap the name. The child concerned stands up so that he can be identified with the name.

The teacher claps various name-rhythms each of which the children must recognise as belonging to a certain child.

A name (Sheila, Peter, Andrew) is once more spoken and clapped simultaneously by the children.

The teacher plays a recorder melody over the top and the children must maintain the pulse.

The children speak and clap once more, this time without melody, and they must notice whether they get slower or faster.

Instead of a name the rhyme 'Rain, rain, go away, little Johnny wants to play' is spoken over evenly clapped crotchets.

Instead of clapping they use patschen with both hands simultaneously. The patschen is first practised separately and then together with the speech.

The verse is spoken once with clapping and the next time with patschen (dynamic variation).

A small sequence, for instance:

first: forte with clapping,

second: piano with patschen,

third, forte with clapping.

This is done first with the teacher and then tried without him; he only gives the initial start.

Alternating patschen and clapping is practised.

At a sign from the teacher they stop and start again.

With a lengthy practice those children who come out sit out for a time so that after listening and watching for a while they can start afresh.

Relax the hands, arms and shoulders.

Try to speak the rhyme 'Rain, rain, go away' again with the same accompaniment as before.

The children stand up, relax their trunk and legs, run freely about the room to the teacher's accompaniment and, at a call from the teacher, they try, without interrupting their running, to form a large circle. As the teacher's accompaniment gradually slows down so they gradually come to a standstill.

Standing as they are try the rhyme once more with the clapping and patschen accompaniment.

To finish—skipping freely about the room.

Further suggestions for the slightly more experienced:

After reaction exercises at the beginning of the lesson: play with various spatial formations and various ways of moving, again in the form of reaction exercises.

—from a circle to snake formation and back to a circle again;

—simultaneous or alternating movement from several snake formations;

—from a circle to a snail formation (tight spiral) and back to a circle again, galloping in particular shapes determined by obstacles placed on floor;
or:

—turning on the spot in different directions, arms flying freely;

—the same with skipping;

—walking in small individual circles with choice of direction, walking both forwards and backwards without colliding with anyone else;

—the same with skipping;

—walking in small individual figures of eight with choice of direction;

—leading a large figure of eight around two obstacles placed far apart. At first close together so that the halves of the eight do not cross, and then at a greater distance so that the paths cross at the centre and each child must find his way through;

—galloping freely about the room, without touching, to the teacher's melody; when the melody stops they stand still;

—to finish—all children accompany a recorder melody of the teacher's with an ostinato of their own;
or:

173

—echo exercises with clapping or other sound gestures carried out on the spot;
—free rhythmic answering phrases to those given by the teacher;
—making up ostinato patterns with sound gestures to a melody given by the teacher;
—marking time on the spot while giving a clapped ostinato accompaniment;
—walking in a circle or snake formation with a clapped ostinato;
—transferring the ostinato accompaniment to small percussion;
—individual children traverse the room's diagonals while accompanying themselves with a rhythm of their own choice;
—skipping forwards and backwards while moving freely about the room;
or:
—working at one way of moving—skipping for instance—in the form of reaction exercises, then in a simple sequence that can be developed, individually and in pairs, along the diagonal and across the centre of the room, observing a particular sequence of entries (after two bars or after one);
—the support of each entry given by a beat on an instrument (triangle, woodblock, bass drum) at first given by the teacher and then by a child;
—changing the spatial formation;
—changing the way of moving or the movement sequence;
—to finish—free improvisation from all the children or in smaller groups in the way of moving that has been practised with clear starts and finishes, the whole exercise led by a melody from the teacher.

174

Appendix

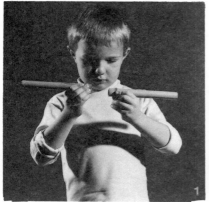

Claves (or rhythm sticks) are used in pairs. They should be made of a hard wood with a good sound, or of sections of bamboo approximately 20 cm long and 2–3 cm in diameter. These bamboo sticks can be made by sawing up a longer piece at a point about 3 cm below each node.

Claves are struck at right angles, one upon the other. The bamboo sticks should be held at the noded end. These hollow, noded ends can be struck one against the other to obtain a more muffled sound (Fig. 1).

A brighter sound is achieved through creating a resonance chamber by curling the fingers of one hand into the palm, placing one stick in the shallow channel thus formed, and striking it in the centre with the other stick (Fig. 2).

A tremolo can be achieved with bamboo sticks by holding two of them in a 'V' shape and with a third stick travelling rapidly backwards and forwards inside the 'V' (Fig. 3).

Rattles are made of hollowed-out material such as wood, clay or metal and exotic fruits such as the coconut or

177

calabash, etc. These are filled with small, hard material for shaking, such as different cereals, seeds, shells, gravel, lead-shot, etc. When making these oneself, the best kind of material and the amount to be used has to be discovered through experiment. It is possible to buy various kinds of rattles in the shape of boxes, gourds and bamboo sticks. (Fig. 4, from l. to r. shows tambourine, sleigh bells and maracas.)

Rattles can be shaken or they can produce a more precise pattern. This latter is achieved through a small, exact, almost rigid movement of the holding hand; by striking the rattle with the

They can be made at home by sawing a coconut in half and scraping out the flesh. One strikes the open sides against each other or against some other hard surface.

Castanets are used in Orff-Schulwerk in the form where one pair is attached to a handle. They can be shaken or, when an exact rhythm is required, they can be held in one hand and struck against the flat palm of the other (Fig. 5).

Woodblocks are made in rectangular shape out of hard wood, with one or two hollowed-out resonance chambers. They can be struck with hard beaters made from felt, rubber or wood. The

other hand; or by striking some other surface, such as the hand or knee, with the rattle itself.

Sleigh bells are made with little bells that are sewn on to a leather or elastic strip. They are either shaken or made to sound through the free hand striking the hand that holds them (Fig. 4, centre). They can also be tied to the ankle when they will emphasise the beat of the wearer's feet.

Coconut shells are particularly useful for giving the effect of horses' hooves.

best place to strike them is near the outside edge, directly over the middle of the resonance chamber (Fig. 6).

The woodblock can be held in one hand and is, therefore, useful as an instrument that can be played while moving. For quick passages it must be fixed to a stand, or placed upon a suitable flat surface and played with two beaters.

Playing upon several woodblocks at different pitches gives a particularly attractive sound.

178

Tubular woodblocks are made from two connected, hollow, wooden cylinders of different pitches. They can be struck with the same kinds of beaters as other woodblocks. They can be held in one hand, or attached to a stand, and are particularly useful as an accompaniment to movement. The best places to strike them are at either of the two extreme ends (Fig. 7).

Triangles should be secured with a fine, strong thread, preferably made of gut or nylon, so that they cannot twist, but the fingers should not touch the metal. The beater is made of metal, and for delicate sounds a steel knitting needle can be used (Fig. 8).

The tremolo is achieved through a rapid zig-zag action with the beater, across the inside of the top angle.

Cymbals as used in Orff-Schulwerk come in sizes from 25 to 35 cm in diameter. They can be used as a pair, or singly.

In pairs: For a sharply accentuated sound in a loud passage the cymbals are clashed with a swift up-and-down movement, one against the other, or with a

6

8

7

9

179

circular movement in each hand, the cymbals meeting at the point where the hands come up together. The sound can be allowed to ring freely, or can be damped through pressing the edges of the cymbals firmly against the clothes. To achieve a quiet sound, the cymbals are held as close to one another as possible before being struck together. Another way of playing: The rim of each cymbal can be struck one against the other when held at right angles (Fig. 9).

Singly: The cymbal can be attached to a stand or can be held by the leather strap. It can be played with various

Finger cymbals have a diameter of 4–5 cm. They are supplied with an elastic and should be placed on the end phalanx of thumb and middle finger, so that they can be clashed with a rebound one against the other. They are very useful as an accompaniment to movement. They can also be held one in each hand and gently stroked one against the other, with an up-and-down movement (Fig. 11).

Hand drums or tambours have single skins that are stretched over a narrow, cylindrical frame with tension screws. (The versions with nailed on skins are

beaters made from different kinds of felt, wood or steel. It can also be struck in different parts, near the dome or near the rim (Fig. 10). It can be struck by the handle of a stick held vertically against the rim. Cymbal rolls are executed with two beaters playing near the edge. On no account should cheap cymbals be used; their tone is brassy and does not combine well with the sounds of the other instruments.

Small cymbals are used in a similar way to the above but have a smaller diameter.

not recommended, for they do not allow the tension to be varied.) The screws should hold the skin at an even tension, and should be tightened before use and slackened after use by the children themselves, so that they learn to handle them properly.

Tambours for children are made in sizes of about 25–50 cm in diameter. They can be struck with soft felt sticks or with the hand. More variety of sound is achieved with the hand. The main areas for striking are the muffled sounding centre of the skin and the

180

brighter sounding area near the rim.

It is advisable to begin by playing near the rim which is easier. The drum is held with the skin in a vertical position, pointing slightly outwards and at waist height. The drum should be held by the frame, not stiffly, but firmly enough to prevent the drum from swinging from side to side when struck. When playing near the rim use the outside three fingers that should strike with a rebound. For this only the fleshy finger pads (not the tips) strike near the rim at a place that is near to the body. The fingers have no individual movement; all movement comes from the wrist (Fig. 12).

This finger action is practised with different tempi and dynamics, at first without accents, later with; at first in unison and later in changing groups.

The deeper kind of sound made with the thumb arises through striking the centre of the skin. This is achieved by allowing the fleshy part at the base of the thumb to come first into contact with the skin, closely followed, through a rolling movement, by the rest of the thumb as far as the tip. It is important that the soft sound of the thumb base and the harder sound of the thumb itself should merge into *one* sound. The hard sound, that is so often to be heard, arises when only the thumb strikes the skin (Fig. 13).

This rolling thumb action also comes from an elastic wrist action; the thumb should not slide across the skin, nor should the tips of the other fingers touch the skin.

Both finger and thumb action are practised slowly in regular alternation, and then faster and in freer structures.

Tambours are particularly suitable

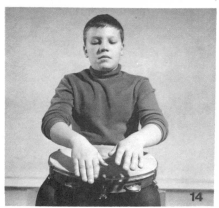

for all forms of movement accompaniment.

Other ways of sounding the drum, such as a single finger on the rim, 'stopped' sounds with a flat hand on the skin centre, circular stroking of the skin with the palm of the hand, scratching with the finger nails, should be tried out individually.

Striking with both hands is possible when seated, with the drum held between the knees (double ended drums with two skins are also suitable for this

way as the tambour, or can be made to sound through shaking, striking on the rim or on the wooden frame of the vertically held instrument. Quick alternation between both hands is possible when the instrument is placed upon the knees (Fig. 14). For strong accents the tambourine is struck against the knee.

Bongos are cylindrical or conical single skinned drums that are attached to one another in pairs of differing size and pitch. The skins are tensioned with screws. Bongos can be held between the knees or placed on a stand. They are

technique). At first thumb and finger action can be practised simultaneously with both right and left hand, and then complementary patterns in all possible time structures and rhythms are practised.

Later it will be possible to play an ostinato with one hand while the other plays a free rhythm.

For a further variety of sound let one hand play with a soft, felt-headed stick.

The **tambourine** is a tambour with pairs of free-moving jingles built into the frame. It can be played in the same

struck with a straight index finger, or with index and middle finger together in such a way that both skin and rim are struck simultaneously (Figs. 15 and 16). Because of their two different pitches bongos are particularly suitable for the accompaniment of exercises in movement that are aimed at reaction training.

The **bass drum** is a double-skinned drum with a cylindrical frame that has a diameter of 50–60 cm, whose skin is tensioned by means of a screw mechanism. It is played with large, soft beaters, sounds muffled when played in the centre and brighter near the rim. It has a strong reverberation (Fig. 17).

The **timpani** used in Orff-Schulwerk are of special construction that, smaller than those used in orchestras today, match the amount of sound produced by the other Schulwerk instruments. They are built as kettle drums with metal bowls and natural skins (today plastic skins that are not so sensitive to atmospheric changes are also often used) and have a central tuning mechanism. Their timbre is metallic in character. Each instrument has a compass of about one sixth.

Cylindrical wooden timpani are also used. These are made with or without central tuning, and have a vibrating and not so precise tone, similar to that of the bass drum. Each instrument has a compass of about one fifth.

In addition, small and medium-sized Baroque kettle drums that are frequently available can also be used. They have no tuning mechanism, but have an especially full sound and are particularly suitable for large ensembles.

The skin of the timpani should be struck about a hand's breadth from the edge. Soft, felt sticks are mostly used. The prerequisite for a well-rounded timpani tone is a rebounding stick action with a loose wrist. The sticks are held in the same way as for barred instruments (Fig. 18).

Timpani are the only tunable skin instruments whose parts are written in staff notation. The entire compass of all the different available sizes of timpani ranges approximately from D to g.

In some cases the traditional position for timpani is with the larger drum to the right, but the reverse is also possible.

This latter position corresponds to the arrangement of bars on the barred instruments and is preferred for Schulwerk.

Barred instruments comprise xylophones, glockenspiels and metallophones. Experience shows that they stimulate children's desire to make music in a special way, through being easy to play in the early stages. The most suitable for starting are the xylophones, made especially for Schulwerk, with their gentle, unprovocative sound. (The bars are laid on a resonance box that

183

The barred instruments (diatonic with extra F♯s and B♭) as used in the first stages of teaching are:

Bass xylophone*	Compass: C–a	Notation	Sounds:
		 *(notation on staff)*	1 octave lower
Alto xylophone	Compass: c–a′	Notation as above	as notated
Soprano xylophone	Compass: c′–a″	Notation as above	1 octave higher
Alto glockenspiel	Compass: c′–a″	Notation as above	1 octave higher
Soprano glocken-spiel	Compass: c″–a‴	Notation as above	2 octaves higher
Alto metallophone	Compass: c–a′	Notation as above	as notated
Soprano metallo-phone	Compass: c′–a″	Notation as above	1 octave higher

increases the tone, and they are struck with felt beaters, whereas the earlier form had no resonance box and was struck with wooden beaters.) The possibility of placing on the instrument only those notes that are needed helps the player to find his way more easily.

All barred instruments are available in the combined alto and soprano form as well as in the chromatic form. Prospectuses of the types offered are available through the retailers.

Beaters: for bass xylophone—hard felt or wound round with wool; for alto and soprano xylophone—hard felt or, for a particularly sharp sound, with wooden heads; for alto and soprano glockenspiel—with wooden heads; for alto and soprano metallophone—hard felt.

* The bass xylophone, that was not mass produced at the time of the appearance of the first Orff-Schulwerk books *Music for Children*, has meanwhile established itself everywhere and is especially suitable for children's music making. In most cases it can be used as a bass instrument with a simple fundamental accompaniment. It can also be called upon as a substitute for timpani or bass part.

Instructions on the technique of playing barred instruments are to be found in the chapter 'Disposition and posture when playing barred percussion instruments' in the section 'Melodic Exercises', p. 60 ff.

For **musical glasses,** wine glasses and tumblers that sound well can be assembled from one's own resources. If those of the exact pitch cannot be found, then glasses that are too sharp can be tuned as much as a semi-tone lower by adding water. The glasses are struck with a rebound by wooden-headed beaters near the upper edge (Fig. 19).

A special way of playing them is by rubbing round the rim with a moistened finger tip. This produces a sustained, penetrating, singing tone.

Recorders are of special significance in Schulwerk teaching for their ability to sustain a melody. The different types of recorder, their ranges, playing technique and possibilities for use are so widely known today that no instruction is required here. For its use in Schulwerk teaching see the chapter 'Hints on the early stages of recorder playing' in the section 'Melodic Exercises', p. 95.

Guitars (or lutes if available) are used as plucked string instruments. The strings are often tuned to a suitable ostinato, in order to achieve a fuller sound that is not restricted by being held down by the fingers. In this way many accompaniments can also be played by children who have had no previous experience of this instrument. A particularly cutting sound is achieved through striking the strings with a plectron or a wooden stick (beater handle).

As a sustaining bass for the performance of drone bass accompaniments a low-pitched string instrument is used, for which a **violoncello** (or gamba) are most suitable. This part is always designated 'Bass'. The strings can be bowed (arco) or plucked (pizzicato) or, to achieve a special sound, they can be struck individually with a felt stick.

The drone bass instrument, called Bordun, specially built for children, can also undertake this function (Fig. 20).

Photo: STUDIO 49

The Orff-Institut

The Orff-Institut is a department of the 'Mozarteum', a university for the study of music and the performing arts in Salzburg, Austria. Founded by Carl Orff in 1961, its function is the artistic and pedagogical training of teachers for Music and Dance Education. It offers, apart from the four-year diploma course, a two-year postgraduate course for applicants with a teaching diploma in music, dance or general education. Every other year there is a one-year course in English entitled 'Advanced Studies in Music and Dance Education – Orff-Schulwerk'.

Affiliated to the Orff-Institut is the 'Institut für musikalische Sozial- und Heilpädagogik', a centre concerned with research and teaching in various aspects of special education.

Every year the Orff-Institut organises International Summer Courses (in German and English) for Music and Dance Education with a varying focus. Information about these courses can be obtained from: Orff-Institut der Hochschule 'Mozarteum', Frohnburgweg 55, A-5020 Salzburg, Austria.

Orff-Schulwerk
Carl Orff/Gunild Keetman

Orff-Schulwerk (Music for Children) presents a fundamental, preliminary study for acquiring knowledge and understanding of music and language.

German Edition (1950-4)

Band I: *Im Fünftonraum*
Band II: *Dur – Bordun/Stufen*
Band III: *Dur – Dominanten*
Band IV: *Moll – Bordun/Stufen*
Band V: *Moll – Dominanten*

SUPPLEMENTARY VOLUMES

Paralipomena (Carl Orff)
A miscellaneous collection of material – works not included in the original edition, later compositions which reflect the developments of new forms, and the use of new instruments.

Lieder für die Schule, Vols 1-7 (1, 3, 5 and 7 Gunild Keetman, 2 and 4
    Gertrud Willert-Orff, 6 Carl Orff)
A selection of folk and children's songs in the German tradition with instrumental accompaniment.

Rhythmische Übung (Gunild Keetman)
Further exercises using sound gestures (clapping, stamping, etc.).

Erstes Spiel am Xylophon (Gunild Keetman)
Songs and pieces for the earliest stage of xylophone-playing.

Spielbuch für Xylophon (Gunild Keetman)
Book 1 (one player)
Book 2 (two players)
Book 3 (two-octave xylophone, one and two players)

Spielbüch für Blockflöten (Gunild Keetman)
Book 1: Fifteen pieces for two to four recorders.
Book 2: Thirteen pieces for two to five recorders.

Stücke für Flöte und Trommel (Gunild Keetman)
Book 1: Twenty pieces for one descant/soprano recorder and hand-drum, and
    twelve canons for two descant/soprano recorders and hand-drum.
Book 2: A further twenty-six pieces with more complex rhythms.

Spielstücke für Blockflöten und kleines Schlagwerk (Gunild Keetman)
Nine pieces for two to five recorders and percussion.

Spielstücke für Kleines Schlagwerk (Gunild Keetman)
Twelve pieces for small groups of mixed percussion.

Üb-und Spielstücke für Pauken (Gunild Keetman)
Exercises and pieces for one to four timpani including some for two players using three timpani each.

Einzug und Reigen (Carl Orff)
A processional piece and a dance for recorders, mixed percussion and plucked string instruments.

Klavier-Übung (Carl Orff)
These piano pieces build upon the elementary principles of the Schulwerk.

190

Geigen-Übung (Carl Orff)
Book 1 (for solo violin, with suggestions for easy accompaniments)
Book 2 (for two violins)

Bläser-Übung (Hermann Regner)
Exercises and pieces for brass instruments, solo and ensemble.
Book 1 (solo and ensemble)
Book 2 (ensemble with occasional percussion)

Stücke für Sprechchor (Carl Orff)
Pieces for speaker, speech choir and percussion.

Cantus-Firmus-Sätze (Carl Orff)
Ten old melodies for three-part voices or instruments.

ENGLISH LANGUAGE EDITIONS

American Edition

Music for Children 1: Pre-School
Music for Children 2: Primary
Music for Children 3: Upper Elementary

SUPPLEMENTARY VOLUMES

All Around the Buttercup (Ruth Boshkoff)
The folk-song arrangements are organised progressively, each new note being
introduced one at a time.

Circus Rondo (Donald Slagel)
A stylized circus presentation using music, movement, speech and improvisational
technique, for various Orff instruments, recorders and voices.

Eight Miniatures (Hermann Regner)
Ensemble pieces for recorders and Orff instruments for advanced players which
lead directly from elementary 'Music for Children' to chamber music for recorders.

Fence Posts and Other Poems (Ruth Pollock Hamm)
Texts for melodies, 'Sound Envelopes', Movement and Composition. New
material for creative melody-making and improvisation including jazz.

Four Psalm Settings (Sue Ellen Page)
For unison and two-part voices and Orff instruments.

191

Have You Any Wool? Three Bags Full! (Richard Gill)
Seventeen traditional rhymes for voices and Orff instruments. Speech exercises. elaborate settings for Orff instruments using nursery rhymes to show how to play with texts.

Kukuriku (Miriam Samuelson)
Traditional Hebrew songs and dances arranged for voices, recorders and Orff instruments. Instructions (with diagrams) are given for the dances.

The Quangle Wangle's Hat (Sara Newbury)
Edward Lear's delightful poem, set for speaker(s), recorders and Orff instruments (with movement and dance improvisation).

Recorders plus/1-3 Orff Instruments (Isabel Carley)
A series of three books designed to fill a need for a repertoire (pentatonic and diatonic) for beginning and intermediate recorder players. Most of the pieces are intended to be both played and danced. Simple accompaniments for Orff instruments are provided.

Simply Sung (Mary Goetze)
Folk songs arranged in three parts for young singers.

Tales to Tell, Tales to Play (Carol Erion and Linda Monssen)
Four Indian, African, German and American-Indian folk tales retold and arranged for music and movement, with accompaniment for recorders and Orff instruments.

Ten Folk Carols for Christmas from the United States (Jane Frazee)
Settings of Appalachian and unfamiliar carols, arranged for voices, recorders and Orff instruments.

Wind Songs (Phillip Rhodes)
Four songs for unison voices, and barred and small percussion instruments.

English Edition (Murray)

Music for Children (Margaret Murray)
Adaptation in five volumes, based on the complete original German edition, including additional English material.

SUPPLEMENTARY VOLUMES

The Christmas Story (Carl Orff/Gunild Keetman)
A play for stage or concert performance, for speaking parts, singers and chorus, with instrumental accompaniments for recorders, strings and percussion.

Eight English Nursery Songs (Margaret Murray)
Traditional songs with instrumental accompaniments.

Eighteen Pieces (Margaret Murray)
For descant/soprano recorder and Orff instruments, taken from Vols. 1 and 2 of "Schulwerk".

Wee Willie Winkie (Margaret Murray)
Eight songs using three and four notes with easy instrumental accompaniments for Orff instruments.

Nine Carols (Margaret Murray)
Settings of well-known carols for Orff instruments, recorders, cello and guitar.

English Edition (Hall, Walter)

Music for Children (Doreen Hall and Arnold Walter)
Adaptation in five volumes, based on Vols. 1, 2 and 4 of the original German edition, including additional American and Canadian material.

Teachers Manual (Doreen Hall)
A concise booklet helping the teacher to develop the ideas and material presented in the five volumes.

SUPPLEMENTARY VOLUMES

Carols and Anthems (Isabel McNeill Carley)
Book 1 and 2. Mostly extracted from the Hall/Walter and Murray main volumes of *Schulwerk,* in the original instrumentation.

Nursery Rhymes and Songs (Doreen Hall)
Twelve songs for Orff instruments, recorders and guitar.

Singing Games and Songs (Doreen Hall)
Twelve traditional songs with Orff instruments.

Songs for Schools (Keith Bissell)
Nine well-known folk songs for voices (unison, two and three part), and Orff instruments.

Sayings-Riddles-Auguries-Charms (Gertrud Orff)
Studies for speech

EDITIONS IN OTHER LANGUAGES

Orff-Schulwerk has been translated and adapted for use in many countries and there are editions in numerous languages, with a comprehensive range of supplementary material.

African

African Songs and Rhythms for Children (William K. Amoaku)
Orff-Schulwerk in the African tradition; a selection from Ghana, based entirely on African material.

Bolivian

*Orff-Schulwerk en Bolivia Y Otras Actividades Musicales en la
    Escuela* (Maria Luisa A. de Williams)
One volume each for the teacher and the student. (Published by Impreso Sucre, Bolivia)

Brazilian

Cançoes das Crianças Brasileiras (Hermann Regenr)
Ten folk songs and dances for children with accompaniments for recorders and Orff instruments.

Czech

Ceska Orffova Skola (Ilja Hurnik and Petr Eben)
Adaptation in 3 volumes
(Published by Editio Supraphon, Prague)

Danish

Danske Børne – Og Folkesange (Minna Lange-Ronnefeld)
Thirteen folk songs for recorders and Orff instruments.

Dutch

Muziek Voor Kinderen (Marcel Andries and Jos Wuytack) Adaptation in 4 volumes
Nederlandse Volksliederen (Marcel Andries)
Nine Flemish folk songs with accompaniments for recorders and Orff instruments.
Elf Nederlandse Volksliederen (Jos Wuytack)
Eleven old Flemish songs with accompaniments for recorders and Orff instruments.

Estonian

Koolimusika − Ansamblimängu Aabits (Heino Jürisalu)
Koolimusika Eesti Rahvalauludest ja Pillilugudest (Veljo Tormis) (Published by NSUL Muusikafondi Eesti Vabariiklik Osakond, Tallinn)

French

Musique pour Enfants (Jos Wuytack and Aline Pendleton-Pelliot)
Adaptation in 3 volumes
Chansons Originales Francaises (Gunild Keetman)
Ten French songs from the complete edition (unison and two parts) for Orff instruments and recorders.
Chansons Enfantines (Gunild Keetman)
Fourteen original French songs for voice with Orff instruments and recorders.
Dix Chansons Françaises (Jos Wuytack)
Ten French songs with accompaniment for Orff instruments and recorders.

Greek

Greek Songs and Dances for Children (Polyxene Mathéy)
A unique collection of original songs and dances from the mainland and the islands of Greece. The text of the songs is given in Greek script and modern phonetic Greek. Accompaniments for Orff instruments and recorders.
Book 1 (with detailed dance instructions in German) and Book 2

Italian

Musica per Bambini (Giovanni Piazza)
Manuale (a handbook for the teacher)
Esercitazioni Pratiche (Practical exercises and examples)
(Published by Suvini Zerboni, Milan)

Japanese

Several volumes based on the Orff/Keetman German edition (adapted by Nachino Fukui) and the introduction to *Musik für Kinder* by Keller/Reusch (translated by Seiji Haschimoto)
(Published by Ongaku-No-Tomo, Tokyo)
Orff-Schulwerk − Theory and Practice (Yoshio Hoshino)
(Published by Zen-On, Tokyo)
Further volumes adapted by Yoshio Hoshino and Thoru Iguchi.

Korean

Orff-Schulwerk — Korean Edition (Chung, Chung-Sik and Myeung, Ja Hwang)
(Published by Edition Seoul)

Latin American

Musica Para Niños (Guillermo Graetzer)
Adaptation in 4 volumes
Introducción a la Practica Del Orff-Schulwerk (Guillermo Graetzer and Antonio Yepes)
Further volumes adapted by Guillermo Graetzer
(All published by Ricordi Americana, Buenos Aires)

Portuguese

Musica para Crianças (Maria de lourdes Martins)
Adaptation in two volumes
Canções para as Escolas (Maria de Lourdes Martins)
Ten popular Portuguese songs.

Spanish

Musica Para Niños (Montserrat Sanuy and Luciano Gonzales Sarmiento)
Adaptation in one volume
(Published by Union Musical Espanola, Madrid)

Swedish

Musik för Barn (Daniel Helldèn)
Adaptation in two volumes
Ung Kyroton (Carl Orff/Gunild Keetman)
Twelve spiritual folk songs for voices with instruments (2 volumes)
(Translation: Knut Waldmar)
(Published by Carl Gehrmans Musikförlag, Stockholm)

Taiwanese

Orff-Schulwerk — Taiwanese Edition (Lin, Jong-Teh)
Adaptation in 3 volumes
Taiwanese and Chinese Childrens' Songs (Gunild Keetman and Lin. Jong-Teh) In 2 volumes
(Both published by Hwa-Ming, Tainan)

Welsh

Music for Children — Welsh Edition (Eleanor Olwen Jones)
This volume closely follows the *English Music for Children Vol.I (Murray)*
substituting Welsh for English wherever words are used in speech or song.
Chive Cân Werin Gymreig (Eleanor Olwen Jones)
Six Welsh folk songs for Orff instruments, recorder and guitar.

GRAMOPHONE RECORDS (IN GERMAN)

Musica Poetica

This series of ten LP records with accompanying notes in German, English and
French presents a documentation in sound and a model interpretation of excerpts
and pieces from the five volumes of the original German edition and some of its
supplements, including *Paralipomena*.
Harmonia Mundi: LP1-5: HM 1C 153-99 885/89
　　　　　　　　 LP 6-10: HM 1C 153-99 890/94

Orff-Schulwerk 'Musik für Kinder', Part I and II
Harmonia Mundi/Electrola (Dacapo): VP 2103-2104

Die Weihnachtsgeschichte — Weihnachtslieder (Carl Orff/Gunild Keetman)
Harmonia Mundi/Electrola: 1C 057-99 658

Bibliography

Böhm, Suse: *Spiele mit dem Orff-Schulwerk,* Photographs by Peter Keetman, Stuttgart, 1975

Hall, Doreen: *Teachers Manual,* Mainz, 1960

Haselbach, Barbara: *Dance Education: basic principles and models for nursery and primary school,* London, 1978,
Improvisation, Dance, Movement, St Louis, 1981

Keller, Wilhelm: *Introduction to 'Music for Children'* (translated by Susan Kennedy), London, 1986

Orff, Carl: *The Schulwerk,* Volume 3 of Carl Orff/Documentation 'His Life and Works', an eight volume autobiography by Carl Orff (translated by Margaret Murray) New York, 1978
'Memorandum' (Proposals for the inclusion of *Orff-Schulwerk* in German schools), Orff-Schulwerk Society Bulletin (England), No.8, July, 1966
'The Schulwerk − its origins and aims', Music Educator's Journal (Canada), No.49, April/May 1963; *Also in* Music for Children − Musique pour enfants (Canada), Bulletin No.21, Summer, 1982

Orff-Institut Publications:
Yearbooks 1962 (also in English), 1963 and Yearbook III (1964-1968), edited by Werner Thomas and Willibald Goetze, published by Schott, Mainz
Documentation '10 Jahre Orff-Institut', Salzburg, 1972
Documentations 'Symposion Orff-Schulwerk' 1975, 1980 and 1985 respectively (with English translations and summaries)
'Informationen', the twice yearly information bulletin of the Orff-Institut gives reports on the progress of Orff-Schulwerk at the Orff-Institut and in many parts of the world.

Orff Schulwerk Societies in the United States of America, Australia, Austria, Belgium, Canada, France, German Federal Republic, Italy, Netherlands, Southern Africa, Switzerland and the United Kingdom publish information bulletins regularly.

'Orff Re-echoes', selections from the *Orff Echo* and the Supplements, 1969-75, edited by Isabel McNeill Carley, American Orff Schulwerk Association, 1977

'Orff Re-echoes II', selections from the *Orff Echo* 1975-83, edited by Isabel McNeill Carley, American Orff-Schulwerk Association, 1984

Orff-Schulwerk: Background and Commentary, articles from German and Austrian Periodicals, collected and translated by Mary Stringham, St Louis, 1976

Orff, Gertrud: *The Orff Music Therapy,* active furthering of the development of the child, (Translated by Margaret Murray) London, 1974
Schlüsselbegriffe der Orff-Musiktherapie, Darstellung und Beispiele, Basel, 1984

198

Thomas, Werner: *Musica Poetica. Gestalt und Funktion des Orff-Schulwerks,* Tutzing, 1977

'Bibliography of materials in English concerning Orff-Schulwerk', compiled and annotated by Mary Stringham, *Orff-Echo* (U.S.A), Supplement No.11, 1977

Index